Twayne's United States Authors Series

Sylvia E. Bowman, *Editor*

INDIANA UNIVERSITY

William Dunlap

WILLIAM DUNLAP

by ROBERT H. CANARY

University of Hawaii

 164

Twayne Publishers, Inc. :: New York

FOR MORE THAN ONE RICHARD CANARY

Preface

As a dramatist, a theater manager, and a painter, William Dunlap played an important role in early American cultural history; as a biographer and historian, he recorded much about the early artists and writers that would otherwise have been lost. In any era, such a figure would command attention. Dunlap demands it especially because of his place at the beginning of our history as a nation. He was not merely the leading dramatist of his time but our first professional playwright, not merely an important theater manager but the first non-actor to occupy such a post in America, not merely an important painter but one of the founding members and first officers of the National Academy. In no field did he achieve greatness, but the variety and importance of his contributions make it impossible to speak of his era without taking Dunlap into account.

Despite Dunlap's achievements, it has been more than fifty years since the last full-length study of him appeared. A number of scholarly articles dealing with special aspects of his life and work have appeared in recent years, but his work is rarely found in anthologies of American literature, and it seems likely that his work is little known by the general reader. The critical analysis of Dunlap's work can scarcely be said to have begun. Dunlap has something to offer the reader and critic as well as the literary historian. This study attempts to show the wide range of Dunlap's work, to indicate what part of it is of continuing interest to the general student of American literature, and to suggest the directions literary analysis of it must take.

Because Dunlap is not widely known, Chapter 1 is devoted to his life. It sets forth one major theme of this study: Dunlap as a representative of the artists who made a place for the arts in the new nation. It also offers some new suggestions about the roots of Dunlap's character, which is present in all of his works and often the only interesting thing in them. Since this study is basically a literary one, Dunlap's career as a painter is treated only briefly, as it bears on his writings. Readers who wish a complete account of Dunlap's life should consult Oral Sumner Coad's *William Dunlap* (1917), a critical biography now available in a reprint edition. Chapter 2 presents Dunlap's two most important works: his histories of American arts and the American theater. Although written late in his career, these works are closely related to his life and set forth the critical principles which govern his work. Chapters 3 through 5 deal with Dunlap's plays, his most important purely literary products. Chapter 6 discusses a variety of minor works, and Chapter 7 is an attempt at a final evaluation.

For my first introduction to Dunlap the dramatist and Dunlap the art historian I must thank Napier Wilt and Joshua C. Taylor. I owe thanks as well to John R. Adams for the encouragement to undertake this work. For comments on the manuscript I am obliged to my colleague Malcolm Nelson and my editor Sylvia E. Bowman. The San Diego State Foundation supported the research for this book with two travel grants. For permission to use and publish material from their manuscript collections, I am indebted to the Boston Public Library, the Historical Society of Pennsylvania, the Massachusetts Historical Society, the New York State Library, the University of Virginia, and Yale University. I have also been blessed with helpful librarians at Grinnell College, San Diego State College, and the University of Chicago.

ROBERT H. CANARY

University of Hawaii

Contents

Chronology

1800   *The Knight of Guadalquiver* and translations produced.

1801– Two patriotic interludes and several translations produced.
1802

1803   *The Glory of Columbia—Her Yeomanry!* and *Bonaparte in England* produced.

1804   *Conceit Can Cure, Conceit Can Kill,* and *Lewis of Monte Blanco* produced.

1805   Goes bankrupt; retires with family to mother's farm in Perth Amboy. Becomes itinerant portraitist.

1806   Returns to New York theater as assistant to Thomas Cooper. Undertakes to publish his collected plays.

1810– Travels with George Frederick Cooke for Cooper. Leaves
1811   Cooper's employ to resume painting.

1812   *Yankee Chronology* produced.

1813   *Memoirs of Cooke* published. Publishes five issues of magazine, *Monthly Recorder.*

1814   Begins service as assistant paymaster-general of New York militia. Publishes two historical treatments of Napoleonic wars.

1815   *Life of Charles Brockden Brown* published.

1816   Service with militia ends. Resumes painting career.

1822   Shows first exhibition picture, *Christ Rejected.*

1827   *The Flying Dutchman* produced.

1828   Last translation, *Thirty Years,* and last play, *A Trip to Niagara,* produced.

1830   Appointed Lecturer in Historical Painting at National Academy.

1831   Elected vice-president of National Academy.

1832   *History of the American Theatre* published.

1833   Receives $2500 from testimonial benefit.

1834   *History of the Rise and Progress of the Arts of Design in the United States* published.

1836   Novel, *Memoirs of a Water-Drinker,* published.

1837   *History of New York, for Schools* published. Daughter Margaret dies.

1838   Declines re-election to National Academy post because of health.

1839   First volume of *History of the New Netherlands, Province of New York, and State of New York* published. Dies September 28; buried in Perth Amboy.

William Dunlap

CHAPTER 1

The Bankrupt Artist

IN THE course of a long and financially unrewarding career, William Dunlap earned the titles posterity has granted him: "the Father of the American Theater" and "the American Vasari." There were painters and playwrights in colonial America, but the Revolution marked an important change in the cultural conditions facing American artists and intellectuals. Like the cultural leaders of today's new nations, Dunlap and his contemporaries were called upon to find or to create an identity for a nation, while they themselves still looked to the mother country for instruction and models.[1] In some respects Dunlap and his fellows had the harder task; unlike many of the newly independent states of Asia and Africa, the United States had no pre-colonial high culture to serve as an alternate model.

Dunlap wrote for a stage which still featured English actors in a largely English repertoire; like most painters of his generation, he studied his art in London. The American audience for art was small; and, like the artists themselves, it was unsure of the value of the native product. It was not an easy life that Dunlap chose for himself, but it won him an honorable place among those who helped make it possible for their successors to create a truly American culture. The representative character of Dunlap's career may be clearer if we see him as one of the first Americans to play out an age-old story: the spoiled son of a well-to-do merchant succumbs to the fatal attractions of the arts and ends as a bankrupt artist.

I *Samuel Dunlap's Son*

A life full of poverty and hardship only mellowed William Dunlap. His lack of bitterness may be his most lovable trait, but it means that we must use with caution the autobiographical accounts he gives us in his histories of American art and American theater. These are our most important sources for his life, but they were written by a man in his late sixties, and they speak of a younger self "so dissimilar" that Dunlap could "with difficulty realize *sameness*." [2] The Dunlap who wrote them had learned to accept the ways of the world, but as a youth he was restless and eager for change. He could have become a prosperous businessman; he chose to become an artist. Many of his associates were ideological conservatives; Dunlap developed radical political and religious views and held to them most of his life. He was destined for prosperity but chose a life that led to failure; and he does not tell us why.

Dunlap was an only child in an era of relatively large families. It may be significant, then, that his first produced play was called *The Father* and later retitled *The Father of an Only Child*. It was the business which his father left him which Dunlap deserted for the theater. We would like, then, to know more of his relationship with his father. He tells us his first memories included being carried while sick in his father's arms, but he tells us little else. On the record, Samuel Dunlap must have been a man of unusual ability, something of a self-made man. A merchant's son himself, he came to North America as a British soldier, rose to the rank of lieutenant, then sold his commission to settle down and marry in Perth Amboy, New Jersey. He prospered well enough as a shopkeeper to maintain the family's Perth Amboy home after their removal to New York City. In New York, he did well enough to be able to indulge his son William in three years of study in England. Samuel Dunlap's only son was blind on one eye from the age of twelve, and he spoiled him. That much we know, but we do not know how well Samuel Dunlap understood his son or what he thought of his artistic inclinations.

There was another man in Perth Amboy who treated Dunlap like a son, even to remembering him in his will, and whose virtues Dunlap records with more emotion than he shows in passages dealing with Samuel Dunlap. Thomas Bartow had been an active figure in New Jersey politics when younger; but, when Dunlap knew him, he was an elderly recluse. Before the injury to his eye, Dunlap had some limited formal instruction from schoolmasters and tutors, but it was Thomas Bartow who taught him to love books. Even before the boy could read, Bartow would sit with him and leaf through illustrated volumes of Homer, Virgil, and Milton, giving the future imitator of Benjamin West his first taste of historical painting. As they looked at the pictures, Bartow would explain the tales they illustrated, giving Dunlap an early foundation in classical legends and history. Later, he gave the boy access to his personal library.

Dunlap's first memories may have been of Samuel Dunlap, but "the happiest moments of childhood" were spent with this second father (*Arts*, I, 245). When Bartow left Perth Amboy at the start of the Revolution, Dunlap followed him to his point of embarkation and stayed until told to return home. The older man died some five years later, and the boy never saw him again. But so sharply did he feel the loss that "Through a long life his image has visited my hours of sleep—always changed—generally sick—or insane—or confined to his chamber and forbidding my approach to him" (*Theatre*, II, 43). From these ghostly visitations Dunlap "awoke, like Caliban, with the disposition to weep for a renewal of my dreams" (*Arts*, I, 246). Images of separated fathers and sons recur in Dunlap's works; with the estrangement from Samuel Dunlap they suggest may be mingled the loss of Thomas Bartow. Dunlap did not become a soldier or a businessman like his father; he spent the money his father left him to enter the world of art first glimpsed in the pages of Bartow's books.

As a former British officer and as an importer, Samuel Dunlap was a loyalist; as his son, William Dunlap was early exposed to the conflicting loyalties produced by the Revolution. He was too young to understand the issues of the war, but old enough to be impressed by its miseries. From Perth Amboy, British regiments marched out bravely; wagons of wounded and dying returned at nightfall. His family, who withdrew from Perth Amboy when it was left in rebel hands, finally settled in New York. Here he saw his first play, performed by British soldiers, and painted his first oil portrait, one of Admiral Hood for a sailors' tavern sign. But, by his own account, he had become a fervent patriot.

As befitted one who had left his native state for New York, Dunlap's patriotism was from the first focused on the nation rather than any one state; like many others, he found a living symbol of its unity and ideals in the charismatic figure of Washington. Like Thomas Bartow, Washington, the father of his country, represents more than Samuel Dunlap the ideals chosen by

William Dunlap for his own. Like Thomas Bartow, Washington is remembered in passages breathing more emotion than is usually found in Dunlap's autobiographical remarks. After the war, the restless young man set out alone for Philadelphia; walking between Trenton and Princeton, he encountered the "man on whom every thought centered" (*Theatre,* II, 52). As Washington rode by, Dunlap "gazed as at a passing vision" (*Arts,* I, 252). Friends arranged an opportunity for Dunlap to paint Washington's portrait and thus mingle more intimately with the great man. Congress was then in session at Princeton, and there too Dunlap had friends. Years later the scenes witnessed then remained in Dunlap's mind like "glowing pictures . . . illuminated by a summer's sun" (*Arts,* I, 251).

A new nation was born, but any young American who wished to be a painter still had to go to England to study what Joshua Reynolds had done and what Benjamin West was doing. In May, 1784, the indulgent Samuel Dunlap sent his son to England to study under West, an expatriate American whose studios were always open to aspiring countrymen. Dunlap took with him some samples of his work, including a full-length picture of Washington on the battlefield at Princeton. Thomas Bartow had shown him that a world of art existed; Samuel Dunlap was willing to pay his passage; the Washington picture was to be his ticket of admission.

But the wanderlust that had led to Dunlap's encounter with Washington was as important in his decision to go as any desire to learn his art. His specimens and some sketches done on his arrival earned him permission to study at the Royal Academy. He did not do so. He delivered a portfolio of drawings to the porter, but never entered the building. For two years he took some instruction from Robert Davy, in whose house he lodged; then he left Davy and took no more formal instruction. His preparation for his London adventure had included attending a dancing school and frequenting New York's billiard parlors. In London, he pursued these interests more diligently than his painting. In the first year he had the excuse of a serious illness; thereafter, his abandonment of more serious pursuits can best be explained as the exuberance of a young man on his own in a great city, well provided with convivial friends, adequately provided with money, and free of any immediate responsibilities. Having escaped his father's authority, he did not hasten to replace it with even the looser discipline of the Academy.

Dunlap was about the age of our present-day college students and far more independent; it should not surprise us, then, if life in London sometimes sounds like a scene from a Sigmund Romberg operetta: some ten years later, Dunlap remembers "that having learned a new song & sung it with the applause of my companions, I, after singing it at the club in the Strand near Charing-cross, went, tho' pretty late, to the Bucks-lodge at the pewter platter near Holborn in the hope of being asked to sing. And many a time have I sate & listen'd to stupidity & ribaldry in the shape of song or story in the impatient hope that my turn would soon come" (*Diary*, I, 51). Dunlap himself suggests that he failed to enter the Academy because he was "too bashful and awkward to introduce myself" and "too timid to ask Mr. West to introduce me" (*Arts*, I, 257), although it required excessive diffidence to remain so shy of West, whose studios he continued to frequent and whose son Raphael was one of Dunlap's boon companions. The pictures and plays he saw in England, both so much better done than any he could have found in the United States, must have provided an education of some value; but his own later judgment was that he had wasted his time. Samuel Dunlap evidently came to suspect as much, for a ship captain suddenly appeared in the son's chambers to announce that the father had booked his passage home. In August, 1787, he left England, never to return.

Back home, Dunlap continued to be a young man about town and a dilettante. He set up a studio in his father's house, but he received few commissions to begin with and fewer still as time wore on. As it had in England, the theater fascinated him more than painting. Spurred by the success of Royall Tyler's *The Contrast*, Dunlap wrote a comedy and had it accepted by the managers of the resident American Company. The production was postponed repeatedly, and the play was never performed because, he discovered, it lacked suitable parts for one of the actor-managers and his wife. Having had this educational contact with the realities of the theater, Dunlap fashioned *The Father* more carefully. It was accepted and performed four times in 1789; he chose to consider this an encouraging run. That fall Dunlap sup-

plied the theater with two prologues and an interlude. Marriage
and the birth of his first child temporarily checked his involvement with the theater; to provide for his family, Dunlap mastered
his previous distaste for business, and the father's business became
Samuel Dunlap and Son.[3] But a few years later, after his father's
death, Dunlap returned to the theater with several plays and
some dramatic criticism published anonymously in the *New York
Magazine.*[4]

Although Washington was a regular attender, many still
thought the theater immoral. Dunlap was sustained in this and in
other literary and intellectual interests by a small circle of like-
minded friends. Samuel Mitchell, met in England, introduced him
to the Philological Society, where the serious discussions led Dunlap "to a more regular course of study than I had ever known"
(*Arts,* I, 267). When it dissolved, he joined some of its ex-
members in the Friendly Club. The members of this organization
were mainly business and professional men, but their discussions
were fairly severely limited to intellectual topics. All too aware
that New York was still an intellectual province of London, they
did their best to be current with British opinion.

After 1793, Charles Brockden Brown was a frequent guest at
these meetings and became one of Dunlap's closest friends. Dunlap took Brown into his home to nurse him through a serious illness and several times had Brown visit him at the family home in
Perth Amboy. Influenced by Brown and mutual friends like Elihu
Hubbard Smith and William Johnson, Dunlap wrote and published poems as well as plays. He was to be active in groups like
the Friendly Club most of his life; his membership in more convivial groups, like Black Friars and Masons, ceased with his marriage.

Dunlap's marriage was evidently a happy one, although he tells
us little about it. It allied him with an old and conservative New
York family, the Woolseys. One brother-in-law was Timothy
Dwight, a "walking repository of the venerable Connecticut
status quo."[5] Dunlap's memoirs speak politely of the pleasure
and intellectual advantages of evenings spent with Dwight, the
future president of Yale; but his diaries for 1797–98 indicate that
he was in firm, though mainly silent, disagreement with Dwight's
political and religious views. He thought Dwight's two "sermons
against Infidel Philosophy: An intemperate farrago of falsehood

and abuse" (I, 264). With obvious contempt, Dunlap confided to his diary the anecdote of a schoolmaster who called on Dwight to ask of a book on natural philosophy not whether it was correct but whether it was on "the right side" (I, 170). On one visit to the Woolsey family, Dunlap found himself, a "poor Infidel philosopher," preaching the virtues of turning the other cheek to pugnacious Federalist Christians (I, 292).

Dunlap's own religious views may have been influenced by the memory of Thomas Bartow, who "read the Bible, but . . . never went to church" (*Arts*, I, 246). The most immediate influence was probably his circle of friends, who urged the joys of philosophy upon him and chided him for his occasional "allusions to the Vulgar cant of the religionists." [6] Even James Kent, who later called Smith "a terrible freethinker," [7] remarked in the Friendly Club "that men of information were now nearly as free from vulgar superstition or the Christian religion as they were in ye time of Cicero from the pagan superstition" (*Diary*, I, 151). Diary entries indicate that Dunlap accepted the Deist notion of a first cause and did not believe that Christianity was the only true religion. Churchgoers, at least Methodists, he thought "ignorant" and mostly "stupid"; Dunlap preferred to stay at home and read the skeptical philosopher Hume (*Diary*, I, 96–98). He respected Tom Paine and regarded the excesses of religious revivals as "Lunacy" (*Diary*, I, 174, 347). The views Dunlap held were by no means original, but they were unorthodox and certainly not what we might expect from the brother-in-law of Timothy Dwight.

Dwight was a violently partisan Federalist; so were most of the members of the Friendly Club. Even Smith, radical in so many ways, was an extreme Federalist. It would seem likely that Dunlap, a son of a British soldier and one who had spent three happy years in England, would cast his own lot with the pro-British, anti-French party. Some remarks in Dunlap's plays have been taken to reflect these views, but the direct evidence of his diaries shows that he did not share the anti-French prejudices of men like Dwight. Dunlap was repelled by the violence but was willing to believe that the Revolution had led to good and that France was "obliged to act offensively towards the world for its own preservation" (I, 297). High Federalists regarded the Jeffersonians as Jacobins in disguise and the Jacobins as little more than devils in disguise. In 1797, Dunlap began a novel called "The Anti-Jacobin" in his diary. The title character is an unsympathetic Presbyterian clergyman who equates Jacobin with "innovator, disorganizer, anarchist, antifederalist, heretic, sceptic, materialist, infidel, deist and Atheist" (I, 155).

The presence of "innovator" and "infidel" on this list may suggest Dunlap's reaction to Dwight's poetry; the presence of "antifederalist" shows that he was aware of the domestic political implications. Dunlap was twitted the night before writing this passage for his own *infidelity* (I, 153); he was sympathetic to Deism and would never have equated it with atheism. It is hard to aviod the conclusion that Dwight has provided the basis for the novel's anti-hero. We may wonder if the hero, newly returned from Europe and full of radical ideas, does not owe something to Dunlap himself. If Dunlap had finished this novel, we might have had a fuller exposition of his political views; but he did not do so, perhaps because he was not a party man and did not wish to write a partisan novel. As an admirer of Washington, he may have given his vote to the Federalists who claimed the right of succession, but he was surely accurate in his later remark to Washington Irving that he "had always been a Democrat" (*Diary,* III, 746).

Dunlap also held unconventional views on other social issues. At the Friendly Club, he encountered the writings of the English radical William Godwin. He was especially impressed by Godwin's *An Enquiry concerning the Principles of Political Justice* (1793); in a letter to Godwin's friend Thomas Holcroft, he expressed regret that his first few plays "were written before my mind receiv'd that impulse which is communicated by a clear & undoubting tho' every enquiring philosophy, based on immutable Justice" (*Diary,* I, 118). Dunlap actually tried to begin a correspondence with Godwin, and one of his magazine articles argues the Godwinian position that patriotism should be based on "reason and love of virtue" rather than on emotion.[8] Even before this, he had participated actively in the antislavery movement. He was prominent in the affairs of New York's Manumission Society; in 1797, he served as a delegate to a national convention of such societies. Perhaps he was honoring the memory of Thomas Bartow, who had had the only house in Perth Amboy without slaves. Samuel Dunlap had kept slaves; his son, who had been reared among them, took great pleasure in freeing them after his father's death.

Dunlap was not a strident rebel against his father or against his society. He joined his father in the china and glassware business and carried it on with new partners for some years after his father's death. He kept silent in the face of Dwight's dogmatism; many of the thoughts confided to his diary do not make their way into his writings. Nor was he a bohemian. Having known the pleasures of at least wine and song before his marriage, he put them by afterward and came to care more strongly about the cause of temperance than about the details of religious and political doctrines. Even as a young man, he cared little for intellectual systems but remained admirably open to ideas. He had begun to educate himself, but he was still just a well-to-do young man about town in 1796 when he agreed to purchase a half-interest in the American Company. During his nine hard years of service as its acting manager, he gradually severed his contacts with the business that was once Samuel Dunlap & Son; at the end of those years, he was neither young nor well-to-do. With his inheritance gone, he was to be wholly his own man, an artist by necessity as well as by choice.

II   *The Manager*

When William Dunlap completed his first play, he scarcely knew how "to approach those awful personages, the managers"; he did not realize "how gladly they would meet any overtures from the son of a merchant" (*Theatre*, I, 148). An older Dunlap, looking back, had the advantage of having acquired an intimate knowledge of the attraction money held for actors. It was his money, as much as any skills he might have, which Lewis Hallam and John Hodgkinson sought when they offered to make him acting manager of the company in return for buying half of Hodgkinson's interest. At the end, Dunlap was left alone to face bankruptcy.

The theater in America had attained a somewhat more secure footing than in the immediate post-Revolutionary years. Boston had finally allowed theatrical performances. The American Company now had a major rival, based in Philadelphia and headed by its own former first comedian, Thomas Wignell. It no longer split its salaries according to fixed shares; most players operated on a salary basis, supplemented by special "benefit" performances, in which the night's profit went to the actor whose benefit it was. The actors were often those who had been unable to make a go of it in England; some, however, came to America while still young and grew more skillful as they matured. Control of the company was vested in its managers; until Dunlap's term, the managers had been the leading actors of the company. Their control was limited by the actors' generally recognized right to retain a part once cast in it and to be cast in parts fitting their special "line."

New York was still a small city; few dramas could be repeated many times in succession. This often, perhaps usually, meant inadequate rehearsals and frequent on-stage recourse to the prompter, especially in new plays. But much of the repertory was traditional, and the company must have gained some of the advantages of a repertory company system: familiarity with parts repeated over a number of years, with each other from playing together regularly, and with the audience's normal reactions—all without the staleness of a long run.

In adding the well-connected Dunlap to themselves, the managers may have hoped to consolidate the theater's growing respectability, and perhaps to make use of his contacts with New York's business and intellectual community. But from the beginning Dunlap was called upon to open his pocketbook. John Durang, then a minor actor in the company, later wrote that Dunlap's entrance into the managership kept the theater "prop'd on its foundation"; individual actors were no doubt pleased to discover that "Mr. Dunlap would always assist and advance money to a performer." [9] One of Dunlap's first duties was to travel with the company to Hartford, Connecticut, for the opening of a summer season; before returning to Perth Amboy, he left behind four or five hundred dollars to cover projected losses.

Hallam and Hodgkinson had uses for both Dunlap's respectable associations and his money, but the immediate cause of their offer to him was their need of a third man to serve as a buffer between them. No repertory system can eliminate the natural rivalry among actors for salary and position. Hodgkinson, who had come to America in 1792, quickly won the public's favor; and with this leverage he had taken over principal parts long the property of others. He was successful alike in comedy, tragedy, and opera; and he injured his rivals all the more for this versatility. His wife likewise coveted and secured leading roles. In 1794, John Henry, one of the co-managers, retired from the stage and sold his half-interest to Hodgkinson. Henry felt himself betrayed by his partner Hallam, but Hallam himself soon found Hodgkinson an uncomfortable rival. The ill feeling between them was increased when Hodgkinson forced Mrs. Hallam's temporary withdrawal from the stage, complaining of her habitual drunkenness. Barely on speaking terms, the partners could not agree on such fundamental parts of management as casting. Hodgkinson wanted more and more leading roles; Hallam felt himself and his wife unfairly treated.

Unable to reach decisions between themselves, they ceded authority to Dunlap—but without withdrawing their claims. If their motives in doing so seem clear enough, Dunlap's motives for accepting the offer are less so. He may have been misled about the financial position of the company, but he was familiar enough with its members to be clear about the personality conflicts he would have to deal with. He may have considered his position as a chance to further his career as a dramatist. His ambitions in this direction were encouraged by his friends—Elihu Hubbard Smith, who deemed *Fontainville Abbey* (1795) the best tragedy in twenty years, believed Dunlap might become "the most respectable dramatic author of the age." [10] Faced with a lifetime of shop-keeping as the most likely alternative, Dunlap persuaded himself that it was his moral duty "to take the direction of so powerful an engine as the stage" since, by doing so, "surely I should have the power to do much good" (*Theatre*, I, 287).

"The power of the engine was certain," he learned; "his powers to direct it he ought to have doubted" (*Theatre*, I, 287). The partners' agreement gave Dunlap the semblance of power. Subject to the joint disapproval of his partners, he was to choose which plays were to be performed. With the approval of one, he could enter into contracts and establish rules and regulations, which his partners were bound to respect. Made a part of the initial agreement was one such regulation, prohibiting back-stage visitors except by Dunlap's written permission. In casting Dunlap was given the most explicit authority. He was bound to respect agreements previously made with other performers, and Hallam and Hodgkinson were guaranteed their previously held parts, agreeing in turn to play them when called upon and not to resign them without Dunlap's permission. But Dunlap might choose the new plays he wished and cast them as he liked; his associates might decline a part but could not exercise a veto. Older plays left unperformed under Hallam and Hodgkinson—*Hamlet* was among those specifically named—were also his to cast.

The terms of the agreement seemed favorable, but in the theater power is won and kept at the box office, not in nicely ordered contracts. Dunlap's own plays were no match for his partners' public appeal. Like Henry and Hallam, he was to suffer from the necessity to placate the popular Hodgkinson. Competition with the Philadelphia company and other ventures only improved the bargaining position of the better actors. For example, Thomas Cooper, brought to America by Wignell in 1796, did not play two full seasons in succession with either the New York or Philadelphia companies during Dunlap's managership; he bettered his parts and raised his salary by seesawing between them. Dunlap's power was also sharply limited by the need to find plays with parts his leading actors could and would play, as well as by the need to please a relatively small audience. The economics of the situation made it difficult for Dunlap to impose discipline upon his quarreling company. A more forceful character than Dunlap might have been able to do so, but the genial debates of the Friendly Club had not prepared him for the bitter quarrels of the green room; he knew how to be a good friend, but he had not learned to be an effective enemy.

No doubt Dunlap would have found it easier to maintain the actors' morale if he had not also been faced with a reduced intake and rising costs. Competition, again a factor, restricted the profits to be made by taking the company on tour during the summer. Dunlap was also forced to help pay for his partners' errors in judgment: in the summer of 1797, Hodgkinson again took the company to Hartford and again failed to make expenses; he moved on to Boston, leaving a second company to pacify the Hartford theater owners. As a result, Dunlap helped make up losses for two companies rather than one. Yellow fever epidemics several times forced the elimination of the first and most lucrative portion of the fall season and discouraged attendance even after the theater was open. Failure to secure a properly signed agreement for the use of a new theater on New York's Park Street led to yearly rentals that took up much of the profit of a large house.

As the financial situation worsened, Dunlap's partners left him to deal with it alone and otherwise made it harder to bear. Their feud had continued unabated by his presence. When in disgust he temporarily withdrew as acting manager, the Hallams contrived a dramatic, sudden reappearance on stage of the banished Mrs. Hallam, who appealed to the audience to be allowed to return. Afflicted by the hissing of a claque planted by the Hallams, Hodgkinson renounced the stage. He returned under a new agreement whereby Hallam sold his interest to Dunlap and Hodgkinson and retreated to the relative security of a mere salaried actor. Then in 1798, when the theater proprietors raised the rent, Hodgkinson gave up his half-interest to manage a company in Boston; Hallam could not be persuaded to return to management. Unsuccessful in Boston, Hodgkinson returned to New York as a salaried actor; and his rivalry with Cooper produced more green-room friction and led to the first of that actor's departures. With Cooper gone, Hodgkinson was the undisputed favorite of the audience and turned to quarreling with Dunlap. He demanded expensive perquisites at a time when Dunlap was in no position and of no mind to grant them; nevertheless, Dunlap had to appease Hodgkinson as best he could. In 1803, with Dunlap forced to retrench, Hodgkinson left the company rather than accept a reduced salary, thereby depriving the company of its most popular actor.

Under these conditions, Dunlap's progress into debt was steady. Much of the summer of 1797 was spent in attempts to borrow money to prepare for the coming season. To Hodgkinson he wrote that he was "running about town to borrow, subject to mortifications which almost weary me of life" (*Diary*, I, 144). Unaccustomed to debt, he was upset in part "by the difficulty of borrowing" but "more by the necessity" (*Diary*, I, 143). By 1803, he was forced to mortgage his farm to settle accounts for the recently finished season. By January 1, 1805, at the age of thirty-eight, he wrote: "Oppressed with disease and debt, I commence another year of my life with sentiments of gloom and self-disapprobation." [11] On February 22 the theater was closed, and Dunlap forfeited all of his property to help pay debts. To add to his problems, a New Jersey marshal, for whom he had put up bond, defaulted, placing Dunlap in debt to the federal government. Yet the bankruptcy which forced him back to his mother's home had the merit of extricating him from an impossible situation. At the beginning of the next year he could express relief at being finally free from "a debt which destroy'd mind & body" (*Diary,* II, 363).

Dunlap's bankruptcy was the ultimate proof of his inability to control the engine of the theater; he had already found that its power of doing good was limited. Hoping to present the best in drama, he had found himself hoping to attract the audience with plays he disliked and circus acts he thought degrading to the stage, like that "of a man who could whirl round on his head with crackers and other fireworks attached to his heels" (*Theatre,* II, 151). But, although he failed to raise by much the cultural level of the New York theater, Dunlap has been credited with certain achievements as a manager—improved scenic effects, more frequent production of native drama, and the introduction of Continental drama.[12] Dunlap's part in these developments should not be exaggerated, and it is doubtful whether they justify his suffering.

Much of the credit for the introduction of adequate scenery into the New York theater belongs to Charles Ciceri, a scene painter whose connection with the theater began some three years before Dunlap assumed its direction and who continued with it until driven to resign by Hodgkinson's rudeness. Dunlap later said that he himself was too ignorant "to be of much service in directing the scenic department" (*Theatre,* II, 69). As a manager, he did bring forth a number of pieces which appealed to the audience's love of scenic effects, but he can hardly have thought much of such crowd-catching gimmicks as running streams and burning houses. Spectacle is the least worthy element of drama. But the audiences responded, and the improvements Dunlap left behind him were not the least practical part of his legacy to his successors in the theater's management.

Dunlap did attempt to present more works by native playwrights. He labored hard himself to provide fresh pieces for the company, and from his period as manager the bulk of his work dates. It cannot be said that the reception of his plays very much advanced the cause of American drama. Of the plays not by his own hand, a number would have found their way to the stage no matter who was manager. There was a built-in demand for plays laid in native scenes and celebrating patriotic occasions; despite the lack of prestige or reward for native drama, playwrights would have arisen to fill the need. Of his own work, we may notice that the pressure of time under which he worked forced him to produce many more translations and adaptations than original plays. His original plays in the period show neither decline nor growth. Since a number of his better plays were written and produced before his tenure as manager, it seems likely that he could have continued to have this satisfaction without enduring the burdens of management. He could not have escaped thereby the realities of the theater, but he might have been able to take more risks if he had not had to make box-office success his first priority. Dunlap might have done more for the American drama by remaining a solvent businessman and an independent playwright.

The 1798 success of Dunlap's translation of A. F. F. von Kotzebue's *The Stranger* led Dunlap to translate a large number of plays by Kotzebue and other German playwrights. He also translated and adapted some French farces and melodramas. We may wonder, though, whether the introduction of such fare was a great service to the American theater. Kotzebue is mere *kitsch;* and, as we shall see, few of Dunlap's other translations had even the pretensions to seriousness of Kotzebue, then called "the German Shakespeare." Dunlap, who had no high regard for Kotzebue, regretted that such "attractive novelties" kept from the stage "*Hamlet* and *Macbeth* and all the glories of the drama" (*Theatre*, I, 125). Even the actors grew tired of the German plays. Dunlap's continued exploitation of their popularity was the act of a hard-pressed manager rather than an expression of his own preferences. The Continental drama would have made its way to America even without him. He translated *The Stranger* because it was a hit in London; it required no special enterprise on Dunlap's part to introduce into America dramas already in vogue in England.

It would be ungenerous to deny to Dunlap his title of "father of the American theater" just because so many of his innovations seem in retrospect to have been inevitable; hindsight has its own dangers, and Dunlap earned some sort of title in enduring so much. His bankruptcy ended his most productive period as a dramatist but not all association with the theater. Having taken over the management, Thomas Cooper brought Dunlap back to New York in 1806 as his assistant. The most noteworthy portion of this service was Dunlap's tour with George Frederick Cooke, whom Cooper and his partner had imported from England for the 1810–11 season. Cooke was the greatest actor America had yet seen. He was also prone to appear on stage while drunk, and it was Dunlap's job to prevent this if possible.

"After a sacrifice of another six years" (*Arts,* I, 272), Dunlap returned to painting; but he maintained his interest and contacts in the theater. Each issue of his magazine, the *Monthly Recorder* (April–August, 1813) contains a "Dramatic Record," brief notices of New York performances, probably by Dunlap himself. He wrote a play to celebrate the Battle of New Orleans in 1815, and he wrote several plays for New York's Bowery Theatre in 1827 and 1828. Designed to compete with successes at the Park, they were written "in the plain way of trade, receiving meagre compensation for poor commodities" (*Theatre,* II, 280). In 1833, his contributions to the theater were recognized by a special testimonial benefit, at which Forrest and Kemble starred. Dunlap won this honor as a manager: it is to that period that we owe the bulk of his plays, and it is the hardships of that period which we must bear in mind in judging his achievement as a dramatist. The merchant's son had become an artist and found what vicissitudes awaited those who struggled to create a theater worthy of the new republic.

III   *The Itinerant Painter*

At the very time Dunlap was writing his histories, he spoke of himself as having become "permanently a painter" (*Arts,* I, 274). Yet a later art critic has surmised that Dunlap must have "thought of himself chiefly as an historian and critic." [13] This mistake is instructive, for his history rather than his painting has kept Dunlap's name alive in the works of his successors. Having painted in the period of Benjamin West, Gilbert Stuart, Thomas Sully, and Washington Allston, Dunlap does not assume the same historical importance as a painter that he achieves as a dramatist. Those of us who approach him through his place in literary history may be equally tempted to see Dunlap as primarily a dramatist and historian. It is as a dramatist and historian that he claims our attention, but we must remember that Dunlap was a professional painter before and after his theatrical career. If he did not continue to write plays after his bankruptcy, it was at least partly because he was kept very busy trying to earn a living with pencil and paints. The qualities and problems of Dunlap the painter also parallel those of Dunlap the playwright and helped shape his views as a historian and critic.

Dunlap first turned to painting as a serious profession in 1805. As miniature portraits were fashionable, Dunlap attempted this genre and found that he could make recognizable likenesses. Miniatures were a relatively promising field for a beginning professional. Less expensive and less time-consuming than oil portraits, they offered a wider market, even appearing in such ignoble forms as snuff-box lids and ladies' lockets. Because little more than a likeness was possible in their limited compass, miniatures placed fewer demands upon the artist. Dunlap needed to begin in an undemanding form, for he started with formidable handicaps. His stay in England had left him "ignorant of anatomy, perspective, drawing, and colouring . . . a most incapable painter" (*Arts*, I, 243). Lack of professional training was not his only problem: he had begun as a youth by copying prints, which had made him more aware of the interplay of light and shadow than of color. Although at first he did not suspect it, he later decided that he "did not possess a painter's eye for colour" (*Arts*, I, 250). He was unsure to what extent this defect might be traceable to his partial blindness, which in any case can hardly have improved his potential as a painter. He was to acquire more technical sophistication, but his coloring was always inadequate.

Dunlap's first search for commissions was not encouraging. He journeyed up the Hudson River to Albany, where he found more old friends than sitters. When he moved on to Boston, he arrived there with only the six dollars needed for his week's room and board. The next morning he left some samples at a bookseller's; by the afternoon he had his first customer—for fifteen dollars—and he was soon able to send home some of his profits to his family. This first visit to Boston also brought him instruction; for Edward Malbone, one of America's best miniaturists who was then painting in Boston, showed Dunlap how to prepare his ivory for the reception of paints, saying politely, "I wonder you do so well when your ivory is not prepared" (*Arts*, I, 270). Having once passed up the opportunity to learn, Dunlap spent his professional career learning from his colleagues; and his consciousness of his own deficiencies may have influenced the emphasis on craftsmanship in his history of American arts.

In some respects Dunlap's new career was even harder than his service to the theater, for it required long periods of separation from his family. At the time he entered upon it, even fashionable

portraitists like Gilbert Stuart and Thomas Sully sometimes traveled for commissions. In this first effort, Dunlap based himself in
Perth Amboy. After his first trip north he returned there and then
journeyed south toward Washington, where Secretary of the
Treasury Gallatin assured him he would not be held for the debt
he had incurred on behalf of the defaulting marshal. In the course
of his career Dunlap ranged as far north as Canada and as far
south as Charleston, South Carolina. Until his health failed, his
stamina was remarkable. At the age of fifty-four, he could walk
some nine miles on a frosty Montreal morning to see an old friend,
stay half an hour, and then walk back (*Diary*, II, 563).

Dunlap had a special need to travel, for he was unable to establish himself for any length of time in the major cities. After his
service under Cooper and two years as assistant paymaster-general of the New York militia, he returned to full-time painting in
1816. In 1817 he was appointed keeper and librarian for New
York's American Academy of Fine Arts, of which he was also
elected a director. The post paid two hundred dollars a year and
included a room to use as a studio; but Dunlap, unable to succeed
as an artist, was forced to resign his post in 1819. Because he was
unable to demand much for a portrait, even his traveling sometimes produced little profit. In Norfolk, where he spent the winter
of 1819–20, he noted in December having "begun Eleven portraits
amounting to $315" (*Diary*, II, 494). Some of these may have
been miniatures, but he earlier recorded undertaking portraits of
his host's two daughters at twenty-five dollars each (*Diary*, II,
478). His accounts for the winter's stay show that he sent home
about seventy dollars more than he had brought with him (*Diary*,
II, 534). Although he had had "constant employment" and had
sent some money home, he expected to return to New York "as
poor as I left it" (*Diary*, II, 522).

As age and ill-health made the traveling and insecurity of portrait work harder on his body and spirit, Dunlap made repeated
efforts to find some other source of income as a painter. In 1827 he
sought a commission from Congress for a painting to be hung in
the Capitol building.[14] In 1832 he hoped to obtain the vacant post
of teacher of drawing at West Point.[15] Neither of these efforts was
successful. Dunlap's large exhibition pictures were more profitable. His first was *Christ Rejected*, completed at Norfolk in
March, 1822—a picture based on descriptions of West's picture of

the subject. Dunlap moved it to Philadelphia in June, to Boston and Portland in July. In Portland it took in two to three hundred dollars in two weeks. Later it was sent on tour with an agent, from whom Dunlap occasionally received some profits. He followed this success with three more large-scale paintings. *The Bearing of the Cross* (1824) was less successful on its tour. *Death on a Pale Horse* (1825), another steal from West, earned a good profit and toured as late as 1840, long after Dunlap had sold it. It had been painted in three months, but over *Calvary* (1828) Dunlap labored for three years. He believed it was "very much my best picture," but it was a financial disappointment, and Dunlap had to continue to paint portraits to eat.[16] In 1832, he arranged his four exhibition pictures as a panorama and lectured on them; this was a success until attendance was sharply cut by a spring cholera epidemic, a fate familiar enough to Dunlap.

The derivative quality of Dunlap's exhibition pictures is found also in the plays and suggests a fundamental lack of creative imagination. This defect appears in his painting as early as the picture of Washington at Princeton, done when Dunlap was seventeen. Although Washington was placed on a battlefield, the artist felt obliged to paint him as he had seen him, "in full uniform, booted and spurred"; Washington stood alone, "for the figures in the back-ground I had thrown to a most convenient distance" where much was obscured by "a great deal of smoke" (*Arts*, I, 255). Much later a friendly critic observed that Dunlap sometimes too much neglected "niceties of detail" in pursuit of a "strong general effect." [17] The painting owed a more specific debt to West; it showed "General Mercer, dying in precisely the same attitude that West had adopted for Wolfe—two authors may think alike" (*Arts*, I, 255). For *Death on a Pale Horse* Dunlap used not simply a description but an etching of West's painting. Given a composition to follow and some guide to coloring, he was able to produce fair likenesses by painting from life.

In 1830, Dunlap's pretensions as an exhibition painter were recognized by the National Academy, which made him a lecturer (later professor) of historical painting. Since the position carried with it no salary, it did little to alleviate Dunlap's financial difficulties; but it does indicate something of the respect and affection he received from his fellow artists. Dunlap had been one of the founding members of the National Academy in 1826, when it

broke away from the American Academy, which was dominated
by John Trumbull and the businessmen-patrons of its board of
directors. Dunlap was elected vice-president of the National
Academy in 1831 and re-elected annually thereafter until forced
to resign because of ill-health. His friends in the National Academy were later to encourage him to write his history of American
art; his involvement in its struggle with the American Academy
helped shape his views on the relationship between the artist and
society.

In a free market, the painter can rely on a few individual patrons, while the theater needs large audiences to prosper. It is not
surprising, therefore, that America developed good painters before she developed good dramatists. Painting in an era dominated
by remarkable individual talents, the workmanlike Dunlap
showed talents as a painter of about the same magnitude as he
showed as a playwright; but he did not achieve equivalent distinction. His contemporaries did not value his paintings highly, and
posterity has not been more kind, although in 1954 one Dunlap
portrait brought $6500—more than Dunlap earned from painting
in any year.[18]

In summary, his paintings are like his plays in their derivative
quality and their lack of technical finish: his portraits and water-
color landscapes resemble his histories in their unidealized report-
ing and lack of formal (as opposed to conventional) arrange-
ment. And his career as a painter shows again the difficulties facing
those who chose to make a profession of the arts. Relying on his
slender talent for a livelihood, Dunlap could not help but think of
himself as primarily a painter; safe in our hindsight, we are probably right to value him more highly as a historian and critic of the
art than as a practitioner.

IV   The Survivor

Dunlap's last years were haunted by the possibility of a second
bankruptcy. Perhaps his debts help explain two mysterious diary
entries to which Oral S. Coad has recently called attention.[19] On
June 10, 1832, Dunlap wrote that he was "bow'd down & humbled
by an affliction beyond bearing. Has not my own conduct been
the cause? May God forgive! May my mind be purified by the
thoughts this blow has suggested & may I henceforward do the

will of that God who has decreed that all error must cause sorrow. I may have been the cause unknowingly of this misery, but there are two beings with me who are free from any act or thought connected with that which overwhelms us. How is this?" (III, 601). The two beings mentioned were presumably his wife and daughter. Two days later they were "relieved from a dreadful State of uncertainty & anxiety" (III, 601), but on September 5 he was again "Afflicted beyond measure. O God forgive me—forgive him—help—Why do I write this? Agony is relieved by it a little" (III, 617). An entry for October 23 also notes "Affliction" and "a heavy heart" (III, 626). The heavy heart suggests that the affliction was not physical; in any case, the diaries record matter-of-factly his own and others' illnesses. There is no suggestion of a lasting family quarrel in the surrounding entries. But, if these entries were prompted by debts, their emotional tone is both excessive and not like Dunlap's normal reactions.

Dunlap's more usual state of mind in his last years was expressed some years later in a letter to James Fenimore Cooper, saying he had passed "through so much that I fear nothing: my health is good & I have some good friends." [20] His health was only intermittently good in his last decade, but his friends, including Cooper, sustained him to the end. The amiable nature which had distinguished Dunlap as a young man only ripened under adversity. Said a friendly critic in 1833: "Few men have passed through life so free from reproach and few are so universally beloved." [21] His biographies and histories take their value from his wide friendship among the writers and artists of his day. Dunlap survived poverty and pain to write of those who had shared his hardships and to memorialize those who had not survived.

The friends of Dunlap's youth died young. Elihu Hubbard Smith, a physician, died while carrying out his duties in the yellow fever epidemic of 1798. Charles Brockden Brown wrote that Smith's death "endeared the survivors of the sacred fellowship," Dunlap, Brown, and William Johnson, "to each other in a very high degree," but Brown himself died in 1810. [22] As a young man, Brown was in many ways an uncomfortable friend—moody, depressed with his prospects in life, he sought assurances of affection from his friends. In 1798, he wrote Dunlap complaining that Dunlap had not written him lately. Concluding that Dunlap disapproved of him, he claimed to disapprove of himself; paying his respects to Mrs. Dunlap, he remarks, "I have done nothing to deserve the esteem of your wife. I do not, therefore, expect it. That is no reason why I should not offer her my respect. She is, in the highest degree, worthy of it." [23]

Full of self-reproach but chary of self-revelation, this letter was evidently typical of Brown's letters to his friends. Smith was once driven to write Dunlap: "I have a letter from Charles a few days ago. As usual, it is difficult to learn from it what he is about." [24] Brown's happy marriage and moderately successful career as a Philadelphia journalist and pamphleteer made him less dependent on his friends, although Dunlap's travels kept him in touch with Brown as with others. In 1798, Dunlap could still seem a successful man of the theater; and Brown was just beginning his career as a novelist; in 1805, Dunlap was bankrupt, and it is Brown who apologizes for his failure to answer a Dunlap letter, blaming his domestic felicity and the imminent birth of his first two children (in *Brown,* II, 113–14). But Dunlap was to have the melancholy task of writing his dead friend's biography.

Like Dunlap, Brown had married into a ministerial family; and his opinions grew less radical as he grew more successful. It has been said that Dunlap, too, underwent "a change of heart" (Coad, p. 100) as he grew older, but his opinions underwent no basic change. The evidence for a change is a remark in 1819 that Bible commentaries, by providing alternate readings, might tend to "unsettle belief" in the "unlearned reader" (*Diary,* II, 487). Alone in Norfolk, Dunlap was passing the winter nights by reading through the Bible. Despite this remark, he continued to keep Clarke's commentaries by him as he did so. Other diary entries indicate that he did not take either the Bible or the commentaries uncritically. "The history of these people," he wrote of the Old Testament, "makes them out the most ignorant, stupid, foolish, vile race that can well be conceived of" (II, 493). When the commentary suggested that "When the Bible says God did an evil thing, it is only to mean that he permitted it," Dunlap scribbled: "Where is the difference. If I permit an ill knowing it to be so which I could prevent I am as guilty as if I did it" (II, 490).

Dunlap's own God was a benevolent deity who interfered as little as possible in his creation. To his diary Dunlap confides his doubts about miracles, finding even "The miraculous interference of God" implied by the Resurrection "contradictory to all my notions of God" (II, 495). The regular universe implied by these remarks suggests the continuing influence of the Deistic works he had encountered earlier. Dunlap's diary clearly shows that he regarded Jesus as a good man and an inspired prophet but not as God incarnate, even though he was soon to paint a number of scenes from the life of Christ.[25] Dunlap's published remarks are more circumspect, but they do nothing to suggest that he changed his views later. He certainly thought of himself as a Christian, but his was an ethical Christianity, seeing in the wonders of nature "a confirmation of that religion which teaches love to God and to our neighbour" (*Arts*, II, 259). He continued to reject those who would—like Timothy Dwight—"turn the religion of love into the idolatry of fear" (*Arts*, II, 259). Dunlap's religious views are much like the liberal Christianity of today. They were already less radical in the time of William Ellery Channing than in the time of Timothy Dwight; it was not Dunlap who had changed but his society.

Like his religion, Dunlap's moral and political positions were formed early and held too long. He continued to praise the political philosophy of Godwin (*Theatre*, I, 351). He continued to think of aristocrats as "the humbugs who have kept this world in turmoil since the time of Nimrod."[26] He continued to hate slavery, denouncing "the slave-dealers of Newport" for presuming to think the actor "a greater abomination than the kidnapper, or receiver and abetter of the kidnapper, of the miserable negro" (*Theatre*, I, 42). He continued to regard the French Revolution as "the source of so much present misery and future good" (*Arts*, I, 427).

If Dunlap seems relatively less advanced in these later years, it is because he held to the views of his youth while the world changed around him. The social and political developments of his last decade made him uneasy. Jackson "has proved weaker than could have been anticipated; yet those under him will hold him up."[27] He was willing to support Jackson against the slaveholders of South Carolina, even to the point of war.[28] Street riots he blamed on immigrants: "We go swimmingly here—burn Judges in effigy—and soon hope to burn the laws. A few more cargoes of our folks and all will be in our hands."[29] This uncharacteristically intolerant nativism may be simply an extension of Dunlap's long distrust of the Roman Catholic Church.

Dunlap's distrust of aristocracies, foreign and native, and of mobs, in Paris or New York, comes close to the preference for the "middling" shown by James Fenimore Cooper in his *Notions of the Americans* (1828).[30] Unlike Cooper, Dunlap seems never to have been driven "wild with politics" (*Diary*, III, 792). His letters to Cooper imply agreement with Cooper's politics, but he also professed agreement with Irving, who accepted political appointments from the Jackson administration. In old age as in youth, Dunlap seems long on patriotism and short on partisanship. His moral views, too, were not intolerantly held; indeed, he could hardly have retained so many friends among actors and painters if his hatred of strong drink had intruded overmuch on his conversation. The man his letters and diaries show is very much like the author implied by the histories—a moralistic but tolerant, gossipy but rarely malicious, garrulous old man, living past his time as a sort of charming anachronism.

In writing the histories of American arts and the American theater, Dunlap was able to live again in the time in which he was most productive as an artist—a time in which he might still hope for artistic triumph. The other works of his last decade also show this retreat to the past—sketches of Brown and Stuart for Herring and Longacre's *National Portrait Gallery* (1834–39), a novel first published as *Thirty Years Ago*, histories of the early days of New York, and short fiction based on colonial history. He had every reason to wish to escape the present. His wife and daughter were ill; his daughter died in 1837. He himself was under the daily necessity of "medicine and such feelings as a man had better hide." [31] In his last year he complained that age and illness had made drawing difficult for him.[32]

Friends also helped make life bearable. The most important of these was probably James Fenimore Cooper, a friend of Dunlap's since 1823. They corresponded during Cooper's long sojourn in Europe, and Cooper helped arrange for the London publication of the theater history. Less successful but less bitter, Dunlap urged Cooper to express himself less intemperately in print;[33] and he maintained friendships with Irving and others whom Cooper came to distrust or dislike, but he seems to have had a genuine affection for Cooper. In public he defended his friend, complaining that Cooper's career, like Brown's, had been "interrupted by those who have not appreciated his motives or his character." [34] Dunlap even entered into a frontier real-estate investment with

Cooper; the profits, however, did not materialize so quickly as they hoped, and Dunlap soon found himself in financial straits. Cooper helped him by advancing him small sums against the prospects of the investment. "I paid poor Dunlap his $100 to-day," he wrote Mrs. Cooper, "and he lost it in the street—I have just given him another $50, making $150, in all. I hope he may recover his loss." [35]

Dunlap was thus placed in the awkward position of an old man taking money from a younger friend—"my Banker," as he jokingly called him.[36] "If you can put me in the way of grasping 50 more," he wrote, "I think I shall be provided for until our note is paid." [37] Only a month later he needed a hundred dollars more—if Cooper could not help "I must look for somebody else to sponge upon." [38] With the proud proviso that "if ultimately loss occurs I shall have my share of it," Dunlap accepted this help and a later Cooper offer of a monthly advance.[39] This assistance apparently did not continue past October, 1838, if that late; Cooper may well have despaired of ever recovering sufficient money from the investment.[40] After Dunlap's death, the investment itself became the subject of an awkward correspondence between Cooper and Dunlap's son.

No longer in good health and forced to take money from his friends, William Dunlap died on September 28, 1839. Once he had traveled up and down the East Coast in search of commissions; in his last years, illness had narrowed his world once more to the New York he had come to during the American Revolution. When he died, his family took him back to Perth Amboy for burial. The cycle of generations also came full circle: Samuel Dunlap's son had rebelled and become a writer and painter; William's son John helped his father with his last books but was a respectable lawyer with a businessman's distrust of fancy words. The familiar story ends with another cliché: John Dunlap wrote Cooper, "I am little in the habit of writing any other than business letters. You will please to excuse my abrupt and strait-forward way." [41] Perhaps it was just as well John Dunlap was a good businessman; there was little a bankrupt artist could leave him. But William Dunlap left us a body of work which still demands our attention.

CHAPTER 2

The One-Eyed Man

IN JULY, 1833, Dunlap wrote his friend Cooper that he was at work on "My *great work*," the *History of the Rise and Progress of the Arts of Design in the United States* (1834), suggesting that the title should remind Cooper of Gibbon's *Decline and Fall*.[1] Dunlap was no Gibbon, but this work and the *History of the American Theatre* (1832) are probably his two most important achievements, and with them any serious consideration of Dunlap's works must begin. These major histories, important sources for later historians, are also the best guides to the critical principles which helped shape Dunlap's work. These principles and the vague terminology in which they are expressed reflect the commonplaces of Dunlap's day, which lends them a certain representative character, even while it denies them any independent theoretical interest.

The contrast of "Rise and Progress" with "Decline and Fall" is itself representative of Dunlap and of the age for which he wrote. The attempt to memorialize America's earliest artists owed something to the age's effort to create a proper image of the Golden Age that saw the nation's founding. National attention was turning inward, from the struggles of Europe to the conquest of the frontier and to the problem of slavery. For us, the Age of Jackson has its own heroic qualities, but many then saw only the heroic age of the Founding Fathers receding into the past. Jared Sparks and others were bringing together and publishing the papers and lives of the earlier generation. The first volume of George Bancroft's monumental *History of the United States* was also published in 1834; Dunlap, happy "that such a historian" had been found for his country, sent Bancroft a copy of his own work.[2]

Unlike Bancroft, Dunlap was writing of his own generation; and his histories are filled with nostalgia for years and friends since passed away. Embodying the principles which guided him in shaping art out of life, the histories themselves are his last attempts to give form and meaning to his experience. The youth who grew up during the Revolution still voices a fervent patriotism and a hatred of aristocratic presumption. Tolerance and moralism, equally mixed in his temperament, war with each other in Dunlap's evaluations of artists and their works. Old animosities are also present: Dunlap made few enemies in life, but he did not forget them; his occasional malice contributes much to his histories' readability. Such personal idiosyncrasies sometimes make Dunlap a man of limited vision, but there is much we could not know without these histories.

I   The Artist as Historian

Dunlap, aware of his own limitations, calls his works histories "without presuming to place himself in the rank of professed historians" (*Arts*, I, 9). In both works his purpose is essentially antiquarian: he hopes to preserve the facts of history, but he does not pretend to fit them into some final pattern. An old man, he is anxious to "rescue from oblivion" what he knows, lest the history of his time "be swept from the mind of man" (*Theatre*, I, 3). Judged by Dunlap's declared intentions, the histories are successful; for they "place in the hands of the future historian, many valuable facts, which would otherwise have been lost" (*Arts*, I, 13). He does not give any comprehensive interpretation of the facts he records; Dunlap was both an artist and a historian, but his histories are not works of art.

Of the two books, the *History of the American Theatre* has the simpler form and has more to offer the casual reader. Dunlap had once been manager-director of one of America's two most important theaters, and his Old American Company had been the most prominent of the traveling companies in colonial America. He had heard their stories of the early days, and he used these to supplement what information he could obtain from printed memoirs and old newspapers, which he searched for in the library of the New York Historical Society. The pre-Revolutionary era is crowded into the first three chapters, about 10 per cent of the text. Three more chapters bring us through the Revolution and up to Dunlap's *The Father*. From then on, Dunlap speaks with the authority of one who was a regular playgoer, a playwright, a critic, and a manager. He can use his diary to assist his memory. Even in this period, some matters receive special weight—not quite half of the book consists of a detailed account of the New York scene from the time at which Dunlap entered into partnership with Hallam and Hodgkinson until Dunlap's bankruptcy.

Dunlap has been criticized for the resulting disproportions, especially for giving only passing recognition to the Philadelphia company, which was at least the equal of New York's. This criticism misconceives the nature of Dunlap's book; despite its title, the *History of the American Theatre* is essentially a personal memoir; and Dunlap's personal acquaintance with actors and events has made the work of continuing value. The last portion of the book, taking the history up to the arrival of Cooke, already dealt with in Dunlap's biography of Cooke, lacks the unity of the rest of the book, in good part because Dunlap could no longer use his own experience as manager to give it coherence and organization, even though he was associated with the theater in those years. The relative readability of the history also derives from its interest as autobiography.

The nature of the subject matter and his own relative lack of importance in it meant that Dunlap could not use the same personal framework for the *History of the Rise and Progress of the Arts of Design in the United States*. There is a good deal of autobiography in it (especially I, 243–311), but, when Dunlap apologized for its "undue length" (I, 311), he also explained that he knew more of the events of his own life than of those of other men. The organizing principle of the art history is "a chronological series of biographical notices" (I, 13). The obvious disadvantage of this form is that it reduces many sections to a sequence of one-sentence and one-paragraph notices of otherwise forgotten artists. Only the scholar or antiquarian delights in being told that of Joseph Blackburn "all we know is, that he was nearly contemporary with John Smybert, and painted very respectable portraits in Boston" (I, 32). But the form is well suited to Dunlap's gossipy style, and its quick portraits sometimes give us amusing glimpses of the nature and fate of our early artists: John Quidor's "principal employment in New-York, has been painting devices for fire-engines, and work of that description" (II, 308).[3]

Dunlap makes his task more demanding by an inclusive definition of "design": "Building, modelling, painting, engraving, or landscape gardening" (I, 9). Painters naturally occupy the bulk of his attention, and no landscape gardeners are included; but the book does offer appreciations of the work of engravers, etchers, sculptors, architects, sign-painters, button-gilders—and of Robert Fulton's steamboat. This reflects in part Dunlap's wide circle of acquaintances and in part the wide range of activities in which a single artist might be forced to engage in order to survive. It also indicates the craft-oriented view of art Dunlap held; the same fascination with technique is presumably responsible for such nonbiographical contents as a set of exact directions for the painting of miniatures (by Thomas Cummings) and for the mixing of colors (by Thomas Sully).

More research was required for this history, and Dunlap engaged in an extensive correspondence, relying on his friends in the National Academy, personal friends like Cooper, and even autograph collectors who had sought letters from his collection.[4] In general, his friends responded willingly to his requests for information; perhaps, like Thomas Cole, they were not always aware that Dunlap "had the intention of *publishing*" what they wrote.[5] Henry Sargent protested that he was only an amateur and did not deserve inclusion.[6] Washington Allston professed "invincible repugnance to every thing like personal notoriety" but provided information since his omission would reflect unfavorably on Dunlap if unexplained and on himself if explained.[7] Dunlap had a historian's insatiable appetite for facts, and he pressed his correspondents for more of them. "Sully has been very good but he is too general," he complained to a mutual acquaintance, when, asking him to interview Sully, he also asked him to bear in mind that even the first name of a minor artist "is important to one who wishes to be accurate." [8]

Dunlap had two criteria for the information he received: "to be useful it must be entertaining & have the seal of truth on it." [9] It had to be entertaining as well as accurate because the book had to sell if Dunlap were to make any profit. Much of the burden of selling both histories fell upon their author: Harpers agreed to publish the theater history but waited until the subscription list was full and did not exert themselves to help Dunlap fill it. The art history was also printed after a subscription list had been raised, so that Dunlap's efforts were split between writing the history and seeking subscribers for it. In this instance he also made use of his wide circle of acquaintances across the country.[10]

Despite an understandable desire that his volumes be marketable, Dunlap's concern for their accuracy was genuine. In both histories his use of information from correspondents leads to occasional errors; he did not take—or did not express—a critical attitude toward the information supplied by his friends. He was aware of some errors; and, when sending letters along with his books, he liked to note some of the errata in the histories.[11] As late as 1837, he apologized for an error in the theater history caused by taking the word of Lewis Hallam; Dunlap had learned better while working on his history of New York, and he anticipated correcting himself in some future edition.[12]

A concern for accuracy, a need to entertain, and an inveterate moralism made Dunlap willing to publish some facts his subjects would rather not have seen made public. "Of public men—and every artist is a public man," he wrote, "the public have a right to demand the truth" (*Arts*, I, iii). The treatment of John Howard Payne in the theater history was changed at Payne's request (*Diary*, III, 626), but few of those discussed had Payne's advantage of an advance peek at the manuscript. Dunlap therefore anticipated criticism from some he felt had been treated "fairly and even tenderly." [13] "I love truth," he wrote later, "and have proved that I will expose it freely." [14] One angry contributor called the result "a miserable chronicle of mere gossip and scandal," [15] but Dunlap's willingness to expose the truth has made his histories indispensable sources for his successors.[16] At the cost of outraging a few contemporaries, Dunlap left an important record for posterity of his life and times. Others might be better qualified, but "I do not know of anyone better qualified who is willing to undertake it, and such a work is lamentably wanted." [17]

II   *The Search for an Audience*

Dunlap's major histories and his other criticism share certain major critical concerns. This fact is not surprising, for Dunlap believed that "the Fine arts are all of one family" (*Arts*, I, 2–3). In both histories he discusses the need for an American art, the morality of artists and their works, and the degree to which those works provide a truthful representation of nature. Perhaps the most important of these shared concerns was the need to find and hold an audience for native efforts. Many of the marginal comments in his histories deal with the lack of such an audience, the nature of the audience to be sought, and the sort of artist-audience relationship appropriate to a new society.

Post-Revolutionary American artists had difficulty finding an audience because the eyes of America's leisure class were still fixed on England. The artists were called upon to create a new and original American art.[18] By their efforts, Dunlap believed, the way was opened "for the Coopers, Irvings, Pauldings, Bryants, Walshes, Hallocks, Channings" and other favorites of the 1830's (*Theatre*, I, 220). But writers found that rhetorical calls for a national literature were more common than critical praise or financial success for its first authors. In the first years, most of the books sold were British, and so were most of the plays produced. Although painters were soon able to get a living from portrait work, the prestige of the mother country led many to seek their professional training in London. But there they were taught to regard historical painting as the most important branch of the art, and for it there was at first little market in America.

Dunlap has a clear idea of what the American audience should be like. It must include the best classes in the community: "The artist will address his works to the enlightened men who can appreciate their value," a demand which echoes his friend Smith's hope that his *American Poems* would be read by "the scientific and refined." [19] Only the enlightened have acquired the "knowledge, taste, and refinement" to take pleasure in art: "The uninstructed laborer in civilized society is nearly as dead to those objects which fill us with delight, as the savage. But the man who reads—who delights in books—the educated man—*feels* the want of the poet, the painter, the sculptor, the engraver, and the architect" (*Address*, pp. 5–6). "The wise and the good" must frequent the theater (*Theatre*, I, 129); and the painter must look to "the rich man, rich in taste and knowledge, as well as in the gifts of fortune" (*Address*, p. 8). Having such an audience is the only way to insure a respectable, moral art. The painter must paint what he is paid to paint, and the theater manager finds the common man best lured by "the shameful exhibitions of monsters, and beasts, and other vulgar shows" (*Theatre*, I, 412).

These views are those of a republican idealist who has suffered through long winters of theater managing and portrait painting. They do not necessarily conflict with his political faith in the people; for, at the same time, Dunlap could write Cooper advising the novelist to "write more for the million" (*Diary*, III, 635). He does not plead for theater or painting limited to an elite audience; he asks for support in raising the level of public taste. In particular, he does not miss the influence of a court aristocracy, which he blames for the immorality of Restoration drama and for treating painters as servants. His appeals are directed to America's rising business and professional classes. These men had no tradition of supporting the arts, but they held positions of economic and political power in America and were thus the logical audience for American artists.

In Dunlap's view, the new republic demanded not only a new audience but a new kind of relationship between the artist and his audience; for the republican artist would not tolerate an aristocratic "patron." The notion of patronage was a survival from barbaric times, when artists were forced to cling to men with military power for protection. "The brute of the good old times, and the fool of the improved modern day, have thought, and would have it thought, that artists are their inferiors" (*Theatre*, I, vii). Americans who look down on artists have been corrupted by the example of England; in the new, free society, position and profession do not determine moral quality. The condescending attitude of the American Academy of Fine Arts, whose stockholders were "honoured with the term *patrons*," helped to bring on the secession of most of the artists to form the National Academy (*Arts*, II, 278). Dunlap's far from unprejudiced account of this split dwells at length on this point: the artists who withdrew were right to do so, for they were the social equals of the businessmen and better fitted to judge of artistic works.[20] The son of a well-to-do merchant and once a prosperous businessman himself, Dunlap was particularly unwilling to regard more prosperous men as more worthy.

The artist is also responsible for upholding the dignity of his profession. The artist who caters to would-be patrons, as Dunlap feels Trumbull did in the American Academy, is betraying his fellows. In America, "Every artist who has the feelings of a man, or more especially of a republican man, will spurn from him the offer of patronage, as debasing to himself, to his art, and to his country"

(*Address*, p. 7). The artist of genius "belongs to nature's aristocracy, and despises the aristocracy of mere wealth" (*Address*, p.
15). In an egalitarian society, Dunlap does not trust the taste of
the vulgar multitude; but he is anxious that the enlightened rich
not set themselves up as a new aristocracy, convinced like the old
of their superiority to the artists who give them pleasure.

As a theater manager, Dunlap had been shielded from some of
the social snubs experienced by his actors; but his work as a portrait painter had given him personal experience of the artist's
anomalous social position in America. One of his correspondents
seems to have complained that Dunlap was too hard on the merchant class, for in return Dunlap promises that in the future he
will

> do all possible justice to merchants and bankers. You mention a
> portrait of myself in the profession of a merchant; *that picture*
> was bargained for—and beat down—I received a sum for it
> which would not have brought me bread and small beer during
> the time necessary to its completion: if worth no more than my
> poverty induced me to accept for it, the place assigned to it
> among good pictures on the owner's walls, as described in your
> letter, is one altogether too honorable.[21]

In the same letter Dunlap defends his account of the split between the two academies, and he cites passages in which he gives
due praise to wealthy men who have supported art.

Dunlap desires to replace the patronage relationship with a
marketplace relationship—one more appropriate in a republican
country because the buyer and seller "are equals, bestowing and
receiving good" (*Address*, p. 11). Even if there is material aid, the
giver does not become a patron; he is merely insuring the future
gratification of his taste for art. The artist is like any other crafts-
man—"The agriculturalist, the mechanic, the sailor, the cartman,
the sawyer, the chimney-sweeper, need no protection. When they
are wanted they are sought for—so should it be with the artist; at
least let him be as independent as the last" (*Arts*, I, 17). Dunlap
is not lowering the artist to the level of the artisan; he is placing
all skilled trades on the same level. In a similar analogy, Dunlap
compares the artist to the lawyer or the physician (*Address*, p.
10). Nor is Dunlap abandoning his claim that the artist is ultimately of more value than the mere statesman. The issue in these

passages is the proper artist-audience relationship, and experience and the republican principles led to Dunlap to formulate as his ideal a marketplace model.

Dunlap's experience also makes him aware that he is prescribing an ideal rather than describing the real effects of a free-market economy upon the artist. America did not have a large enough audience for her native artists because many men who thought themselves educated and were certainly well-off felt no need of art in their lives. Dunlap believes that those who do feel the need must provide for the artists until their fellows become more enlightened. He also suggests that an association of "wealthy enlightened individuals" or the government should create a subsidized theater, practically noting that such a theater could charge low rates of admission and thus undercut its commercial opposition (*Theatre*, I, 132). Had Dunlap himself been manager of such a theater, instead of the Park Street Theater, "He might perhaps have been entitled to the grateful remembrance of his fellow-men" (*Theatre*, II, 38). The years since Dunlap wrote have tremendously expanded the audience for bad art, but we have found no better way to support the serious artist than the devices he suggests: foundation grants and teaching careers for the young painter, foundation-supported theaters and cultural centers in cities large and small. The New Deal's Work Projects Administration, with its massive support of painters and theater people, was too radical to last; but Dunlap suggested its like over a century before its inauguration.

III *Immoral Artists and Moral Art*

The discussions of artistic morality which appear in both histories reflect both critical tendencies of the time and Dunlap's own moralistic temperament. They add little to the significance or interest of the histories, but Dunlap generally avoids confusing moral and esthetic qualities. His desire that the good artist be likewise a good man flows naturally from his desire to give art a respectable social status. An artist who is a drunkard is a traitor to his guild. The morality of the artist's work also reflects upon his fellows, so "he will only aim, if true to himself and his profession, to give that pleasure which refines, that gratification which virtue approves" (*Address*, p. 3). Of the minor painters mentioned in his art history, we learn nearly as much about their morality as of their works. Dunlap does not comment on Hugh Reinagle's ability as an artist, but he tells us that he was "a man of amiable disposition, correct conduct, and unblemished reputation" (*Arts*, II, 296). He is hard on artists like John Pennyman, who could "have been a good artist and a respectable citizen," but "became a drunkard, and died despised or lamented, according to the feelings of those who were acquainted with his talents or his conduct" (*Arts*, II, 260).

Dunlap is equally ready to report the derelictions of actors, but he forgives them much since so few of them have had a proper American upbringing. In England, most of them began as strolling players, a life too often "an education in the school of folly, thoughtless dissipation, or positive vice" (*Theatre*, I, 365). In America, however, they are expected to assume "a more elevated deportment and conduct" (*Theatre*, I, 366). Those who fail to do so are held responsible for the public's doubts about the profession as a whole, which is an honorable one. Like painters, actors may have benefited somewhat from Dunlap's reluctance to be as open in discussing sexual misdeeds as he is with those attributable to drink.

The insistence that the art itself be moral naturally falls most heavily on the theater. The charge that the theater was immoral was an old one. Dunlap belongs in the long line of those who replied by making the highest possible moral claims for the theater.[22] The charge had to be met, for the theater was then as now subject to the power of state legislatures and city magistrates. One might complain that English novels taught American women "to admire the levity and often the vices of the parent country," [23] but it was difficult to stop their importation. The theater could simply be closed.

Dunlap admits, however, that the theater as an institution has some undesirable characteristics. He especially deplores the section reserved for prostitutes, a practice he blames on English precedents. The theater cannot be a "school of morality" so long as "a tier of boxes is appropriated as a gallery to display the allurements of vice" (*Theatre*, II, 127). Dunlap suggests that the government might require escorts of all ladies attending the theater, save those of unreproachable character. Curiously, he is not in favor of denying admission to known prostitutes; the theater can do them no moral harm and may do them good.

Criticisms of the theater as an institution concern Dunlap less than those of morality of the drama. Here Dunlap's sympathies are often with the critics. He admits that actors and managers have sometimes catered to the mob with obscenity and ribaldry. He condemns authors like the Restoration playwrights for filling their plays with indelicate wit. Even Kotzebue, who had made a great deal of money for Dunlap, is criticized for having "revelled in revolting subjects" (*Theatre*, II, 88). The need to improve the moral tone of the theater is a major argument for a subsidized theater employing a director and company selected for moral as well as artistic qualities. Internal reform he thinks unlikely, for actors think only of popularity and managers only of money. Failing a state-run theater, he favors a licensing system like that of England but one run by good republicans.

Although Dunlap admits that much drama is immoral, he always maintains that the drama and the other arts can be instruments of moral instruction. The ideal theater would "teach the truths of history, philosophy, patriotism, and morals"—and would produce no play not calculated to serve this particular objective. It would teach morality by showing vividly the consequences of good and evil acts: "The pictures of folly, ignorance, or humorous absurdity, alive in the closet, have a double life on the stage" (*Theatre*, I, 2). The sublime sentiments of Shakespeare would reach those who would never take a book from the shelf. The fictions of the novel are defended in much the same way: "The author of the best code of moral law presented to man, taught many of his precepts by parables. He knew that he must attract and hold the attention, before he could instruct." [24] And Dunlap defends the primacy of historical painting by arguing that no other branch of the art can so "fill the mind, like the contemplation of a picture, representing an event on which the destinies of mankind depended,—an event which will influence those destinies to all eternity" (*Arts*, II, 367).

Dunlap assigns art a didactic end, but he does not argue that good morals make good art. The artist's duty to support patriotism and morality is a moral duty, not an esthetic requirement. He accepts the responsibility of entertaining the audience. "Far be it from us to attempt to instruct you," he tells his novel's readers (*Water-Drinker*, I, 46), although he says it with tongue in cheek. He believes that English drama is "rising in purity," but he recognizes that it is "declining in force" (*Theatre*, I, 128). He can praise the stageworthy qualities of Kotzebue's plays while condemning their morality; and, while George Farquhar's *The Beaux Strategem* "now cannot be tolerated," it remains nevertheless a "lively and licentious comedy" (*Theatre*, I, 52). He even admits that the theatrical effectiveness of many Restoration comedies depends on a kind of wit and manners he found immoral. He regrets that the barbarism of Shakespeare's time left his plays marred by indecency, but he does not, like some, argue that these moral flaws are also dramatic ones.[25]

Dunlap also knows better than to believe that only a good man can be a good artist. The highest accolade he can bestow on an actor is to term him one "who both in public and in private life upholds the honor of his country," [26] but he is well aware that "mere respectability in any of the fine arts is ever associated with mediocrity" (*Theatre*, I, 170). Cooke rose above respectability as an actor, although he never attained it as a man, and Dunlap does the actor honor. An amiable man on the whole, Dunlap is not always anxious to find moral flaws in artists and their works. He can not understand those who would censure John Gay's *The Beggar's Opera*, for "the mind that could be injured by such a piece of satire must be weak indeed" (*Theatre*, I, 123). He does not condemn John Vanderlyn for painting a nude Ariadne, which caused a mild scandal when exhibited in New York in 1813, although Dunlap was not normally fond of either nudes or Vanderlyn. He did not think better of nudes when they were presented as religious or symbolic works, writing with uncharacteristic irony: "If you have a great *moral* picture of a naked man & woman, success is certain." [27]

Dunlap's moralism was not only in tune with the times but natural to the man. It gives an anxious and defensive note to the histories, which stress more than seems necessary that the artist does not inevitably beat his wife. But the morality he advocates for artists is not extreme, and in the theater, his objections to the special section for prostitutes and to actors drunk on stage seem unexceptionable enough. His moral views may have colored his accounts of minor figures—with whose work he was often unfamiliar—but he knew the difference between art and morality and was willing to forgive much to a man of talent. He does not belong in a narrow puritanical tradition of criticism; as in political life, he was a moderate reformer, one who wished to make people better but was willing to get along with them as they were.

IV *Sincerity and Style*

In general, Dunlap used morality to judge the social utility of a work of art. In judging its esthetic worth, he asked first whether it gave a truthful representation of nature. This criterion would seem to be related to his own concern for accuracy in the histories, and at times he seems to imply a simple mimetic definition of art. But more than simple accuracy is involved, for his key word "truth" is used to refer to both the representational reliability of the work and to the sincerity of its maker. The criterion of "truth" is thus moral as well as esthetic, and it is not always clear whether Dunlap is criticizing the work for being false, the artist for falsifying, or both. Truth and morality are linked in another way, for "Falsehood causes deformity in the moral picture" (*Arts*, II, 164). And, if morality requires truth, truth may insure morality: "That 'there is nothing more opposed to truth' than plays and romances, is an assertion utterly void of just foundation. Plays, poems, and romances, derive their value and popularity from the true delineation of nature, added to the just sentiments introduced, and the moral inculcated by the fable" (*Theatre*, II, 187–88).

Dunlap's confused mimeticism owes less to Aristotle or any other philosopher than to his experience as a painter and to contemporary theories of painting. He often indicates the imitative nature of literary works by metaphors drawn from painting—true delineation, accurate pictures, just portrayals. There is somewhat more generalization in his treatment of painting itself. Dunlap was naturally exposed to the eighteenth-century views of West's predecessor as president of the Royal Academy, Sir Joshua Reynolds. Reynolds advised both "habitual imitation and continued study of the masters," while holding that "Nature is and must be the fountain from which all excellencies originally flow." [28] Dunlap seems to agree with his friend Gilbert Stuart, who said there was "more poetry than truth" in Reynolds' work (*Arts*, I, 184). Dunlap admired the accuracy of Stuart's portraits and asked for his secret, admitting that he had previously followed Reynolds' advice on the matter. "You can elevate your mind as much as you can," said Stuart, "but, while you have nature before you as a model, paint what you see, and look with your own eyes" (*Arts*, I, 217). Dunlap quotes this advice as valuable, although it did not keep him from slavishly following West in his historical paintings. Reynolds looks beyond nature to great art for ideal forms. Dunlap believes that the ideal forms exist in nature: that we study the works of the masters to learn how to see what is already there.

A truthful representation of nature may then be more than a simple rendering of the surface, but it must be faithful to it. A portrait must be recognizable; it must be "like"; catching nuances of character is secondary, though it is clearly a quality Dunlap admires. He praises Stuart's portraits for giving "an insight into the complexion and effect of nature" (*Arts*, I, 217). He is only amused at Jarvis, who having difficulty copying a Stuart original, pointed to it and said, "I will give you nature. . . . That's not nature" (*Arts*, II, 78). He does praise Jarvis for having studied anatomy, the better to paint. Other portrait painters are praised or slated on the basis of their fidelity to nature. In his love of verisimilitude, Dunlap even repeats the old story of a painting so like its original that bystanders declared "*it was the living man, looking directly at you*" (*Arts*, I, 215). Dunlap adds to the critical confusion by never making it clear how far the portrait painter's obligation to produce a likeness derives from his duty to art and how much from his bargain with the sitter.

Even in other categories of art, Dunlap uses a mimetic criterion. In landscapes, he admires the early work of the Hudson River school, praising its devotion to nature and its exact depiction. Thomas Cole began by making "small, but accurate studies of single objects; a tree, a leafless bough. . . . He had now found the right path, and what is most extraordinary, he had found the true mode of pursuing it" (*Arts*, II, 357). Historical and religious painting seem to demand more creative imagination, but Dunlap believes that the important act in this branch of the art is the "choice of subject" (*Arts*, II, 302). This choice made, the artist need strive only to reproduce the scene as it was. He censors John Trumbull (whom he disliked on other grounds) for violating historical truth by having Cornwallis appear in person for the surrender of Yorktown and for suggesting that the first inauguration of Washington might be rearranged when painting for more impressive effect. "Thus," Dunlap moralizes, "the truth of history is to be sacrificed to effect or flattery" (*Arts*, I, 377).

Dunlap's ideas about art are confused and quite possibly wrong, but it would be a mistake to conclude that they were naïve. He is an unsystematic critic rather than a philosopher of art, but he knows there is a difference between the created imitation and the reproduction of the real object: "If a painter to give brilliancy to a button lays on gold leaf he is no longer a painter, but a gilder, he sinks the Artist to the merchant" (*Diary*, III, 712). In the theater, "the Stage is to reflect Natures Image as in a mirror by imitation and is not raised to exhibit realities." As the flat surface of the mirror reflects the three dimensions of life, so art may be thought of as imitating life by the manipulation of artistic conventions. Changing conventions as well as changing views of life are behind Dunlap's praise of the verisimilitude of works which now strike us as artificial.

Artifice in the sense of technique is an artistic good in Dunlap's vocabulary; but, having defined the arts of design as those of form, he rarely considers formal composition in talking about paintings, just as he rarely discusses plot construction in talking about the drama. This lack of feeling for larger forms is apparent in Dunlap's own work. Where the composition is not borrowed from West or the common stock, Dunlap's paintings tend to fall into a jumble of adequately done details—perhaps another reason why he found the miniature a congenial form. His dramas also often have well-wrought parts forming an incoherent whole.

Dunlap's criticism does recognize formal excellence as "style"— like "truth," this term has more than one meaning. At times it assumes the form of elegance, with its social connotations. An early portrait of himself showing a picture to his parents (1788) has this posed elegance alongside a naïve realism of manner; Dunlap shows himself dressed as a stylish young man about town. In his art history, he praises Stuart's personal "manner, which was that of a well-bred gentleman" (*Arts*, I, 222). About to quote a friend, John Wells, Dunlap praises his "just remarks in a style of elegance, which alone could entitle them to a place in this history of dramatic literature" (*Theatre*, I, 379–80).

Dunlap's love of "truth in painting" makes him prefer a style in which nothing is left *"unfinished"* in detail; the actively busy painting also appeals to his instinct for craftsmanship (*Arts*, II, 164). Stuart, who brought to America a style which did not particularize background objects in a portrait, reduced chairs and draperies to mere swirls of paint.[29] This is an effective style because it focuses attention on the most important element in the picture, but Dunlap, although he thinks Stuart a great painter, regrets that he "sometimes neglected the draperies of his paintings, leaving them in a most slovenly state of unfinish" (*Arts*, I, 218).

Dunlap's failure to understand Stuart's style leads him to an apparent preference for the highly finished style of Thomas Sully, "whose designs, in fancy subjects, all partake of the elegant correctness of his character" (*Arts*, II, 101). The correct and decorative nature of Sully's style may have attracted Dunlap because he was himself incapable of much more than straightforward likenesses. It is hard to tell, on the other hand, whether there is irony meant in his reference to the "high finish" of Charles Ingham's work, which "has made him principally the ladies' portrait painter" (*Arts*, II, 273). In the work of Sully, also a favorite of the ladies, devotion to style (and flattery) sometimes meant less attention to strict accuracy of delineation, though Sully's portraits were always "like." In case of conflict, Dunlap opts for accurate likenesses. In 1797, before his difficulties with Trumbull, he examined some portraits at Harvard and noted, "Mr. Adams is by Trumbull & first did not appear to me like him, but on examination I found it accurate, except the tasty air which the painter diffused over it" (*Diary*, I, 188).

Dunlap makes his bows to fancy style, but he has few evident principles of style, being able to praise the style of painters as different as Stuart, Sully, and Allston. The emphasis on sincerity and accuracy, on "truth" in all its various meanings, is far more characteristic of his criticism and far more like the man. If Honest John Adams is to be painted, let him be painted honestly. If a man (like Cooke) is habitually a drunkard, his biographer should portray him as such for the moral edification of his readers.

V   *The Artist as Critic*

Dunlap's morality is simple and his esthetic principles are
vague, but his taste is catholic. Influenced by convention, prejudiced for or against individuals by ties of friendship or barriers of
enmity, he still praises much of the best work of his day and condemns most of the worst. His taste often rises, therefore, above
the general level of his contemporaries.

Personal friendship may be responsible for Dunlap's ranking
Sully's portraits with those of Stuart; the verdict is not one with
which many would agree today. Dunlap does recognize Stuart as
a "man of genius" [30] and consistently places him at the head of his
profession. Dunlap's preference for the miniatures of Edward
Malbone and the landscapes of Thomas Cole is reasonably in accord with posterity's verdict. In historical painting he defers to the
memory of Benjamin West, whose works, seen by Dunlap when
young and imitated when older, made a lasting impression upon
him. More defensible is his respect for Washington Allston, whom
he ranked near West. Artists associated with the National Academy usually receive better treatment than those who were not; the
former benefit by Dunlap's friendship, and the latter suffer from
his lack of familiarity with their work. This prejudice may be responsible for Dunlap's underrating Charles Peale: in 1783, "I saw
and admired Peale's gallery of pictures, for then I admired everything" (*Arts*, I, 251). Dunlap often notes faults in works by his
friends, but on the whole he errs on the side of leniency and over-
enthusiasm. His judgment of painters is not infallible, but at least
one modern critic has concluded that Dunlap has a better than
average percentage of correct guesses about posterity's verdict.[31]

Dunlap has been accused of being unfair to John Trumbull, for
whom he certainly felt no personal friendship. He does paint
Trumbull at his worst; for he pictures him as a domineering and
malign man, and no allowance is made for the bitterness of Trumbull's later years. Dunlap later claimed that in describing Trumbull's character he had "*extenuated* much and thereby injured myself and the cause of truth," [32] but such charity as he may have
exercised is not readily apparent to the reader. But, although his
dislike of Trumbull as a man comes through clearly, he gives a full

catalogue of some paintings Trumbull gave the Yale gallery; and his annotations are often favorable—of one painting he remarks, "This is a jewel" (*Arts*, I, 392n.). He has a defensible preference for the historical paintings of Trumbull's early years, especially "the beautiful pictures of the Battle of Bunker's Hill and Death of Montgomery" (*Arts*, I, 258), which he mentions again in his novel (*Water-Drinker*, I, 181). His biography of Trumbull occupies more space than that of any other painter, with the natural exception of Dunlap himself. The biography is not a eulogy by any means, but it ends with the observation that Trumbull's military pension is not equal to the merits of the man. His characterization of Trumbull is certainly biased, although possibly correct; but his judgments of the works reflect the opinions of his contemporaries and anticipate those of his successors.

Conventionally enough, Dunlap ranks Shakespeare above all other dramatists. Although his career as a manager does not reflect it, Dunlap rejects most of the mutilations of Shakespeare still common in the theater of his era. His opinions of other British dramatists are found more in his biography of Cooke than in his theater history. He likes Francis Beaumont and John Fletcher and disapproves of major alterations in their plays. He likes Richard Brinsley Sheridan's early *School for Scandal*. In his own age, he likes the slight but entertaining comedies of George Colmon. Understandably, he dislikes Addison's *Cato*. His diaries indicate that he was much impressed with Kotzebue's *The Stranger* when he first encountered it, but he did not think him a great playwright when he was a popular favorite, nor a very bad one when he had fallen out of favor. He considers Schiller "the greatest dramatist of his age" (*Theatre*, II, 97) and deplores the infrequency with which he is produced in England and America. He thinks better of the French dramatists of the 1830's than of their British and American counterparts, although he does not grant them much more than relative excellence.

The theater history's concentration on Dunlap's personal fortunes allows for surprisingly few comments on Dunlap's American contemporaries, but he does reprint letters from James Nelson Barker and Mordecai Noah without comment. His final judgment is that Tyler's *The Contrast* "is extremely deficient in plot, dialogue, or incident" (*Theatre*, I, 137). Dunlap does concede the effectiveness of Jonathan, the low comedian's part which proved

the first in a long line of Yankee characters in American drama;
but he does not believe that inserting a Yankee character makes a
play distinctively American, since "a clown is not the type of the
nation he belongs to" (*Theatre*, I, 162). Dunlap may be jealous of
Tyler's work, the first native play to be professionally produced
after the Revolution, thus cheating Dunlap of a certain place in
history. He is certainly not unfair to a popular spectacle of the
time, John Burk's *Bunker Hill,* which never drew a kinder word
from Dunlap than "vile trash" (*Theatre*, II, 163). Dunlap's comments on his own plays are rather modest, considering how large
a role he plays in his history. He claims for them a few passages
worth preserving, perhaps more than we would grant today, and
he is proud that his plays helped keep his theater alive, but he is
otherwise willing to consign them to oblivion.

At this distance in time it is difficult to evaluate Dunlap's criticism of actors and managers. A contemporary critic suggested
that Dunlap "suffers unforgotten partialities or perpetuated dislikes unduly to influence his mind," [33] but the effects of these are
more apparent in, say, his treatment of Hodgkinson the man than
in his treatment of Hodgkinson the actor. Within the conventions
of his time, Dunlap prefers the more "natural" actors; but he is
willing to admire any actor who can move audiences. His lack of a
sense of over-all form again reveals itself in his tendency to discuss actors' renderings of key lines and speeches rather than matters of over-all characterization. Although he professes admiration
for some actors, he thinks theirs is a hard life and advises young
men against entering it. As an ex-manager who had suffered from
the workings of the star system, Dunlap denounces its influence.
Also as a manager, Dunlap approves of those who wrote dramatic
criticism in his day; some, like Irving, were his good friends,
though not always friendly critics. As a playwright, Dunlap's unfortunate experiences with other managers make him think it
worth noting that Snelling Powell used his plays, "always re-
munerating him honourably" (*Theatre*, II, 190). Without singling
out individuals, Dunlap blames the "necessities and cupidities of
managers" for some of the theater's ills (*Theatre*, II, 359).

In fiction, Dunlap's praise of Brown, Cooper, and Irving indicates loyalty to friends as much as innate taste. His diaries indicate that he read regularly in British fiction—Henry Fielding,
Daniel Defoe, Tobias Smollett, and Sir Walter Scott, whose *Talis-*

man he returned to more than once. Laurence Sterne's name does not appear in the index to the surviving diaries, but Dunlap must have read him when young, since his *The Father* originally bore the subtitle of *American Shandyism* and since his opera *Sterne's Maria* is taken from *Tristram Shandy*. Only a few diary entries indicate much about Dunlap's taste in poetry. Dipping into Samuel Taylor Coleridge and Robert Southey at the same time, Dunlap sensibly decided that Coleridge "is the greater poet" (*Diary*, I, 226), and his moral feelings did not keep him from taking some pleasure in Lord Byron's *Don Juan*. He does not seem to have read poetry frequently.

In the several arts with which he was most concerned, Dunlap's criticism provides "a clear cross-section of the tastes and artistic ideals of enlightened gentlemen of the Early Republic." [34] Occasionally his taste was somewhat in advance of his time, perhaps because he had an insider's knowledge of both theater and art. Not a great critic, he should be given credit for the broad taste that goes with his wide range of interests, for the tolerance that underlies his moralizing, and for the concern with practical problems that tempers his idealism. His criticism helps us understand the ideals by which he measured himself, just as his life should help us understand why it was difficult for him to attain those ideals even within the limitations of his talents.

Dunlap holds up the ideal of an enlightened audience for American art. He tells us himself that he had to appeal to an unenlightened audience or fail; in the end, he did both. Dunlap would like to see art a moral force, but he recognizes that it must give pleasure. Unless we count garrulity as a style, Dunlap is not a stylist in his histories, but he does his best to tell the truth. The vagueness of his critical principles is partially redeemed by the extent to which posterity has approved his critical taste. And, despite his occasional inaccuracies, his histories meet the ultimate test of proving themselves useful to later historians.

CHAPTER 3

Comedy and Farce

"THE APPLAUSE of a theater! The play was printed, and is forgotten," Dunlap wrote of his own *André* (*Theatre*, II, 21). He could have said the same of any of his printed plays. Many of his plays did not even achieve the dignity of print. The historian of American drama must especially regret the loss of Dunlap's first known play, *The Modest Soldier*. The first effort, even if unproduced, of an important dramatist is always of some interest. We do know that he was prompted to write it by the success of Tyler's *The Contrast;* and although he tells us he had not seen or read the play when he wrote his own, his list of characters indicates he must have had Tyler's play in mind. Dunlap's "a Yankee servant, a travelled American, an officer in the late revolutionary army, a fop, such as fops then were in New York" presumably derive, respectively, from Tyler's comic Yankee (Jonathan), soldier-hero (Colonel Manly), and foppish villain (Dimple).[1] Dunlap's characteristic imitativeness, displayed in this first effort, sometimes makes it difficult to say which plays are his own. Many of the plays discussed in Chapter 6 as adaptations Dunlap considered original, and most of the plays discussed in this and the next chapter are more or less derivative.

I The Father *and Its Revision*

Although Dunlap wrote more comedies than anything else, relatively few survive. From a historical but not a literary point of view, it is fortunate that among the survivors is *The Father; or, American Shandyism* (1789), the second professionally produced comedy in our native drama—because of the managers' failure to produce *The Modest Soldier*. The debt to Sterne acknowledged in the subtitle is most obvious in the characters of Colonel Duncan and his aide, who play over the battles they fought in during the

Revolution. The loyal Cartridge even tells his master he sometimes thinks "your honour and I are something like Captain *Shandy* and *Trim*, when we are busy in our grass-plot, forming sieges and storming cities" (*Act II*). There is also a widow among the characters, although the Colonel does no more than hold her hand. These three characters also possess a sentimental benevolence which represents the side of Sterne which appeals to Dunlap, but the extravagant form and comedy of impotence which relate Stern to our contemporary "black humorists" find no place in Dunlap's "American Shandyism."

The borrowings from Sterne are largely irrelevant to the plot, which is, however, composed of elements already familiar to Dunlap's audience. As a guardian to a friend's two daughters, the Colonel has married one to a Mr. Racket. In the first act, we learn that Racket is neglecting his business and devoting himself to drink and related evils. Mrs. Racket is endeavoring to make him jealous by encouraging the attentions of his drinking companion, Captain Ranter. The Colonel enters on a surprise visit just as his ex-ward faints in Ranter's arms. The Colonel is shocked, Ranter is insolent, and the lady leaves with Ranter without attempting to explain matters to the Colonel. Can this marriage be saved?

The novice playwright's second act neither complicates the plot nor much advances it. Ranter and the Colonel quarrel, and we hear of the mysterious melancholy and the charitable disposition of Mrs. Racket's sister, Caroline. The only action with any real effect on subsequent events is Racket's telling the maid Susannah that she is to bring him a set of her mistress's clothes that night. Why he wants them is never made clear; his only discernible motive is a desire to get the maid by herself while his wife is at a play. Perhaps Dunlap once thought of having him disguise himself as his wife, to Captain Ranter or someone else.

The clumsy craftsmanship of the second act is somewhat redeemed by the appearance of a comic character, Doctor Quiescent, a pedantic quack. He presents himself as a suitor for Caroline, but he is madly intent on explaining the remarkable cases he has seen and the cures he has made. He is doing his best to make himself known in New York by adopting both of the "two methods of gaining reputation made use of by our physicians. . . . Writing for the news-papers or challenging and caning all the rest of the faculty" (*Act II*). In a preface to the revised version of the play, Dunlap claims the doctor in his time was an "original" character.[2] There may be some original details drawn from Dunlap's medical acquaintances like Smith, but Quiescent is an old comic type. In *The Father,* he has the freshness of originality; he seems to have come to this sentimental comedy from some comedy of "humours."

The playwright is, in fact, as anxious to provoke sentimental tears as laughter. Tender sentiment seems to be the principal aim of the third act, which is mostly taken up with two long expository scenes—exchanges of confidence between Caroline and the Colonel. In the first, she reveals that Ranter has also been courting her—we are never shown this situation, another defect in construction—and the Colonel tells her the story of his life. As a young medical student, he contracted a secret marriage; and, when his wife died and he returned home, he left the boy to be reared by a friendly British officer. Both names appeared on the list of those slain at Bunker Hill. Overcome by emotion, the Colonel leaves Caroline, to allow two comic scenes to vary the pace of the play. In one, Cartridge praises his master to the maid; in the other, the doctor, who thinks he has made a clear proposal to Caroline, assumes he is accepted. In the second expository scene, Caroline explains her melancholy. On a visit to Halifax, she became betrothed to a young British officer; and they planned to marry after the war. His name was Haller; the Colonel, who exclaims that he is his son, is overjoyed to hear he is alive. But Caroline says she has seen Haller's much-prized ring on Ranter's hand. When the Colonel accosts Ranter, he insist he received the ring from his dying friend. The Colonel departs, desolate; and Ranter tells the audience that he feels danger about him and must soon leave.

The plot seems to be about to lead to action when the missing son and lover shows up in the fourth act, but the author keeps him waiting while he contrives some more sentimental situations. Haller, who appears disguised as a blind old soldier, tells Colonel Duncan that Haller still lives; but he does not identify himself, since he does not know and is not told that Colonel Duncan is his father. The happy Colonel and Caroline depart, for no better reason than to permit the author to have Racket and Ranter enter. Ranter, himself trying to borrow from Racket, takes the old soldier for a beggar, tries to throw him out, and is repulsed easily, revealing at once his lack of charity and lack of courage. Racket leads the soldier out, since Dunlap wants to have him off stage when the Colonel confronts Ranter with his news. Ranter says he came on the most direct boat; the soldier, therefore, must have seen Haller before his death. Ranter departs, Caroline weeps, and the Colonel tells his aide to send someone after the soldier and to kept an eye on Ranter.

After some irrelevant dialogue between Racket and Ranter and between the Colonel and his aide, the stage darkens and the action of the fifth act begins—we might almost say, the action of the play begins. Susannah repulses Racket or does her best to do so. They draw back as the doctor enters, planning to "steal softly to her chamber, and tell her *Obadiah Clump* is bit by a mad dog." When the Widow comes looking for burglars and bumps into the doctor, both back off. Ranter and Mrs. Racket return early from the theater, but she will not be seduced, so he seizes her. The Colonel and Cartridge arrive in time, bringing light. In the confusion, Ranter gets the Widow; the doctor, Susannah; and the Rackets, each other. The Rackets are reconciled, Ranter is asked to leave, but the Colonel bars his way and asks again about the ring. Still insisting Haller is dead, Ranter is about to depart when Haller and his friend enter. Ranter, it seems, was actually Haller's rascally servant, who had robbed a master he thought was dying. The father reveals himself to his son, and they embrace. The Rackets embrace; the Colonel brings Caroline, and she and Haller embrace; and everyone forgives everyone else, even Ranter.

The revised version, published as *The Father of an Only Child,* may never have been played; the cast list given is that of the original production, and the play is said to have dropped from the repertory after the departure of Wignell, who had played the comic doctor. Several of the characters are given new names—the doctor (Tattle), the Colonel (Campbell), his aide (Platoon), and the villain (Rushport)—making a discussion of the play more difficult. There are a number of other minor changes, some of them improvements: some topical remarks about the Constitution are omitted, although the recency of the Revolutionary War still dates the play. The Colonel's sending for the old soldier is moved from the end of Act IV to the beginning of the next act, giving him between acts to recover from the villain's insistence on Haller's death—and giving the author a tear-jerking fourth-act curtain. Some irrelevant dialogue at the start of the last act is eliminated. Racket's desire to dress in his wife's clothes remains unmotivated, but the clothes are put to good use in a scene in which the doctor encounters the bundle in the dark and attempts to treat it. The doctor's part, the best thing in the play, is somewhat enlarged.

Other changes, perhaps more fundamental, are of doubtful value; they add to the sentimental moralism of the play without much forwarding the plot. The aide praises the Colonel for freeing his slaves, in a piece of noble sentiment not at all related to the action of the play. The aide fairly explicitly suggests to his master that he should woo the Widow and leave children behind him; this provides a tearful moment for the Colonel, who has married and who believes his son is dead. In the fifth act, Susannah pauses while fending off Racket to deliver a little speech on virtuous conduct between masters and maids, men and women. Her speech convinces Racket he is wrong: "My sight is restored, and I see my own conduct in its true light." Although both his pausing to listen and his being converted are implausible, this change may be excused on the grounds that it prepares for his reconciliation with his wife at the play's end.

The most serious change of all is in the character of Mrs. Racket, one designed to make her morally more acceptable to the audience. Her rather flighty attempt to make Racket jealous becomes the sincere and rational, however mistaken, effort of a desperate woman. She faints in the villain's arms because she assumes it is her husband who comes; and, in the revision, she assures the Colonel before she leaves that she will explain things later. The device is shown as moderately successful. Caroline explains it to the Colonel. In the midst of the villain's attempt to seduce her, Mrs. Racket explains her plan at some length and confesses she now knows "It is my fault that my husband has not been more domestic" (*Act V*).

Among other things, this speech parallels her maid's in improbability, but it does not have so good an effect; the villain's natural resentment of being used now motivates his use of force. But Mrs. Racket's part in the final reconciliation is now fully prepared for. Since the revision gives her one or two fairly witty lines originally her husband's, it is possible that the change in her character reflects the desires of the original actress for a more sympathetic role. The new character is more sympathetic and more rationally motivated, but the speeches and asides which accomplish this effect also slow still more the action of the play. It is hard to say whether or not this and other changes make the revised version an improvement over the original play.

The prologue and epilogue have in either version little to do with the plot, but they cast some light on Dunlap's feelings about the play. The original prologue, like many opening addresses of the period, protests that "The comick muse" has been inspired by her new surroundings to "a serious reformation" of her hitherto often indecent manners. The revised version simply intensifies this theme: the original ends with a plea for indulgence of the "artless muse" of the homegrown author; the revision ends by telling us "we now in Virtue's cause engage,/And rear that glorious thing, a *Moral Stage*." The original epilogue urges the audience to condemn the play even though it is moral and the author young. If it encourages a young writer, it may expect a flood of such unwelcome productions. Evidently Dunlap did not feel overencouraged, for the revised epilogue concentrates on one of his pet grievances; the audience is told to reject the play because it is not by an Englishman: "you'll be undone/If you approve a piece not play'd in London."

The title (or titles) may provide a hint about the meaning of the play. There are other lines of action in the play, but Dunlap singles out the father's search for his son. Strangely enough, this line of the action seems almost imposed upon the play, with which it has little real connection. The Racket's marriage is restored to health without Haller's aid; the Colonel's function in the main plot (initial shock, saving Mrs. Racket) he could perform simply as a guardian. Most of the effect of the conflicting reports on whether Haller is dead or alive could be kept if it were only Caroline who alternately hoped and despaired. Having the Colonel be Haller's father increases the improbability which the audience must accept. That the villain should come wooing Caroline wearing her betrothed's ring is one coincidence, but Dunlap is able to establish at the beginning of the play that Ranter is worried by her interest in it: "I hope she never saw it on any other finger—hang fear of detection" (*Act I*). But the Colonel's sorrow for his son forces the audience to accept another major coincidence, one not brought in until the third act.

The long lost son (or other blood relative) is a stock figure in comedy, but it is interesting that Hallery has two fathers: his supposed father is a British officer, as Samuel Dunlap had been, but his real father is the native-born Colonel. Himself an only child, Dunlap retitled the play *The Father of an Only Child* after his father's death. The phrase appears three times in the revision: the Colonel uses it of himself in Act V. But earlier, the disguised Haller has claimed to be searching for his son; the Colonel calls him "The father of an only child! a long lost, only child!" (*Act IV*). This gives the play two fathers searching for sons.

The estrangement motif appears once more in the villain's explanation of his background, which enabled him to pass convincingly as an officer. His father was a clergyman, and, like Samuel Dunlap, saw to it that his son was well educated. When the son fell among drunken companions and was forced to leave England, his father died of shame. Says the Colonel, "Poor man! He was the father of an only child" (*Act V*). We notice that the good son (Haller) finds that his true father lives; the bad son is responsible for his father's death. The title is used to tie together the three appearances of the father-son theme, all of which are also found in the original. The use of the phrase is an effective theatrical artifice, but the theme itself may have a deeper attraction for Dunlap.

Haller's two fathers, British and American, also represent the mixed cultural heritage of Dunlap and his generation. One way to achieve identity was to reject much of the British legacy; Tyler's *The Contrast* ends with the contrast between the villain, who has "received the polish of Europe," and the hero, "an unpolished, untravelled American" (*Act V, Scene 2*). But having spent three years in England himself, Dunlap could not draw that kind of contrast. In his *The Modest Soldier*, the "travelled American" and the "fop" are separate characters. Reconciliation is Dunlap's characteristic way of resolving conflict, and he is consciously seeking in *The Father* "to soften the asperities which war had created, and to reconcile his countrymen to their English brethren" (*Theatre*, I, 153).

Divided allegiances are, therefore, everywhere: the British soldier loves an American girl, and she loves him; the American Colonel is searching for his British son; even the American Rackets take up with the British Ranter. Love and courage are the virtues appealed to in this sentimental comedy. When Haller is disguised, the Colonel does not care that he was a British soldier; it is enough that he is "a brother soldier" (*Act IV*) in distress. The Colonel and Haller were in opposing armies during the Revolution; now they embrace as father and son. The villain is British, but Haller is the romantic lead who gets the girl, and Haller has been a British officer at Bunker Hill. We may doubt that sentimental comedies have much effect on national prejudices—but we may notice how concerned ethnic groups today are about the images of them projected by the mass media. Whether the play is effective propaganda or not, we may take Dunlap's word for the attempt, for the same theme recurs in other plays.

All in all, *The Father* makes us glad that Tyler's play begins the theatrical history of America. *The Contrast* is not a model of stagecraft, but it is better constructed than Dunlap's play and is also occasionally graced with a wit *The Father* lacks. The sacrifice of probability is deliberate in Dunlap; in a sentimental comedy, plot exists for the sake of producing sentimental occasions. From this point of view, it does not matter that nothing much happens during the first four acts; for the question of Haller's life or death is an adequate substitute. No real plot is needed to bring the Rackets to their senses, for they are basically good. Even Ranter can safely be left to his own feelings of guilt; no punishment is necessary in this all-benevolent world. The Colonel says of a comic German servant, a former Hessian who is not fond of soldiers: "The softening influence of liberty has not yet melted from his heart the scaly crust with which tyranny and oppression had surrounded it" (*Act IV*). Those readers who find themselves tiring of this universal benevolence and ceasing to care whether Haller lives may still enjoy the scene in the dark in the last act, which is effective theater, even if half of the characters have no business being there. And we can see that a good comedian might make something of the comic doctor. No one could wish to see the play revived today, but it is pleasant reading.

II *Two Interludes*

Presumably the success Wignell enjoyed as the doctor in *The Father* led him to ask Dunlap to write the interlude which be-

came *Darby's Return* (1789). The title character of this opening
derivative sketch comes from John O'Keeffe's *The Poor Soldier*
(1782). Wignell was already popular in the role. Dunlap's interlude also draws briefly on the second Darby play by O'Keeffe,
Love in a Camp (1785). These two titles provide a hitherto-
unsuggested source for Dunlap's *The Modest Soldier; or, Love in
New-York.* Among the characters in Dunlap's play were "an old
gentleman and his two daughters, one of course lively and the
other serious" (*Theatre*, I, 147), who may have resembled the
aging Father Luke and his two nieces in *The Poor Soldier.*

The Poor Soldier represents the kind of sentimental comedy
Dunlap tried to write in *The Father*. Darby is the low comic, fond
of drink and a bit of a coward; he loses the lively daughter to a
more handsome, less interesting rival. His story is only a subplot;
for in the main plot, a poor soldier and an officer are rivals for the
serious daughter. What marks this work as a sentimental comedy
is that the officer gives up the girl as soon as he understands the
situation and gives the soldier a commission as a wedding present.
Since the romantic characters are so thoroughly predictable in
their well-intentioned way, the comic characters—the priest, a
French valet, and Darby—run away with the play. Darby's popularity is indicated by the larger role he plays in the sequel, *Love in
a Camp*. In this play he has joined the Prussian army, and his
schemes land himself and others in danger and disgrace, from
which he must be extricated by his own wits and the goodness of
the former poor soldier, Captain Patrick.

Dunlap's interlude opens with some songs from *The Poor Soldier* sung by a chorus of Irish villagers. Darby enters and is
greeted by the girl he lost, by his successful rival, and by Father
Luke. The villagers sing a song asking Darby to tell of his adventures. He tells them that he lost his money in Dublin, thought to
take ship for England, but got "fuddled" and shipped for Danzig
by mistake. This part of the tale comes from *Love in a Camp*, and
he then tells them briefly of his adventures in that play. When the
Turks approached and battle threatened, Darby decided to look
for "an army that was more at rest." He took ship for the United
States, where he was a general favorite—"But more especially I
liked to work/At one nice little place they called New-York." This
couplet may refer in part to Wignell's success in *Darby's Return.*

Darby especially remembers General Washington:

A man who'd fought to free the land from woe,
Like me had left his *farm* a *soldiering* to go;
But having gain'd his point, he had, *like me*,
Return'd his own *potatoe ground* to see.
But there he couldn't rest—with one accord
He's called to be a kind of—, not a Lord—
I don't know what—he's not a great man, sure,
For poor men love him, just as he was poor!
They love him like a father or a brother.

This passage, besides illustrating the quality of Dunlap's couplets, has a special interest since Washington himself attended the first performance of the play and was much observed by the audience as these flattering words were spoken. Washington, who lacked the inexhaustible appetite for flattery of some later Presidents, looked embarrassed. When Darby was asked what Washington had looked like, the President braced himself. "Darby's answer that he had *not seen him*, because he had mistaken a man 'all lace and glitter, botherum and shine,' for him, until all the show had passed, relieved the hero . . . and he indulged in that which was with him extremely rare, a hearty laugh" (*Theatre*, I, 161).

Darby's next journey was to France, where the rioting and violence accompanying the Revolution did not appeal to him. Although his comments are mild, the lines were omitted in performance, perhaps because of the partisan connotations of any mention of the French Revolution at that time.[3] The intent of the lines seems to be to draw a contrast with the orderly change of government in America from the Confederation to the Constitution—"A revolution without blood or blows." The newly married Dunlap may be speaking when Darby says, "But oh, New-York's the place to get a wife,/Aye, that's the place to lead a merry life." Darby has only returned to Ireland for a visit, after which he will return to New York (and the New York stage), "where I'm never seen without a smile." The play ends with a song begging in turn the pit, boxes, and gallery not to be hard on poor Darby.

Washington's laughter made Dunlap remember *Darby's Return* with pleasure. Although he published it, he was fully aware, as he said in his preface, that it was a "Dramatic trifle not written for publication . . . a hasty Production" (p. [3]). No doubt it was an efficient enough display piece for the talents of Wignell. It does have one advantage over *The Father:* its smaller compass permits the dramatist fewer blunders in construction.

Another Dunlap interlude was written for Cooper when the latter was managing the Park Street Theater. *Yankee Chronology* (1812) is actually written around the song of that name, which had earlier been sung between acts by itself. The song celebrates the founding of the nation in the first verse and the events of the American Revolution in the next seven. Washington is again pictured in the most exalted terms, dealing with his foes like the native eagle, "Jove's bird." The ninth verse urges Americans to win again against the same enemy in the War of 1812. Its bombastic tone may be gathered from its chorus: "Then huzza! for the sons of Columbia so free!/They are lords of the soil—they'll be lords of the sea." For those who might be disturbed by the Anglophile word "lords," Dunlap provides a footnote in the printed version, explaining that by "lords of the soil" he means only to convey "that particular felicity of the cultivators of the soil in this country, where almost every man has the fee simple of the land he improves." [4] A tenth verse celebrating the victory of the *Constitution* over the British *Guerriere* was added at Cooper's suggestion, as was an eleventh verse celebrating the anniversary of the British departure from New York on November 25, 1783.

The interlude exists only to provide a plausible reason for having the song sung in character. Two old men, Bundle and O'Blunder, greet the arrival of the former's son, Ben Bundle. Impressed two years previously by the *H.M.S. Outrageous* and never allowed to write his aged father, Ben escaped and made his way to Boston. There he immediately shipped out on the *Constitution*—"and a glorious Constitution *we've* got!—may she ever have a good commander, a faithful watch, and a steady man at the helm." He hoped to give "the enemies of sailors' rights and my own dear country a drubbing," and he was aboard for the victory over the *Guerriere*. At his elders' insistence, he tells them all about it. In an early appearance of an unfortunately characteristic piece of American wartime rhetoric, the father concludes the victory was the work of "the *true* friends of peace." Appended to the printed version of the interlude are two more patriotic songs, "The Freedom of the Seas" and "Yankee Tars." Like the interlude, the tone of these shows that Dunlap was not then overly concerned "to reconcile his countrymen to their English brethren."

The two interludes have a basically similar structure: the extended anecdote with an on-stage audience. The interest resides in the narrative of the person returned from far off (Darby, Ben Bundle). There is no real action. The on-stage audience breaks up the smooth flow of the narrative with exclamations and comic interjections: in *Darby's Return*, a comic old woman mistakes Darby's "Dantzig" for "sea-sick," and a clown keeps asking about whales; in *Yankee Chronology*, the two old men serve as comic foils, making intentional or unintentional puns on the narrator's nautical terminology. Both sketches offer the audience rousing songs; both appeal to patriotism. Neither claims to be more than it is—an occasional piece designed to please a specific audience.

III A Trip to Niagara

Dunlap's last play, like the interludes, is well-done hackwork, *A Trip to Niagara; or, Travellers in America* (1828), a farce. Although it was one of his most successful plays in the theater, Dunlap was not fond of it, and later critics have not been much more favorably impressed.[5] Dunlap's own dislike of the play has obvious roots. In a preface which confesses that the play can pretend to "no higher character" than farce, he tells us the play was commissioned by the managers of the Bowery Theater "as a kind of running accompaniment to the more important product of the Scene-painter," serving "the important purpose of keeping the audience, or spectators, in good humor while the scenery and machinery was in preparation."[6] Dunlap might be a painter himself, but he does not relish playing second fiddle to moving scenery. Perhaps he was led to underrate the play. No doubt it is too much to call it "a social satire that would challenge the ridicule of Ben Jonson"[7]—if the critic who said that meant it as praise—but it is a workmanlike job. It may well be the best of the plays discussed so far—if that assessment can be taken as praise.

The travelers in America are Mr. Wentworth, his sister Amelia, and their servants. Mr. Wentworth dislikes America, but his sister does not. She complains he has been prejudiced by the accounts of earlier English tourists, a sore point for nineteenth-century Americans; he complains she has become "a downright democrat" (*Act I, Scene 1*). To balance their judgments, Amelia's maid misses the class distinctions of England, while Wentworth's

servant likes America so well that he quits Wentworth's service.
After an unsuccessful attempt to hire a Negro waiter, Amelia and
Wentworth employ Denis Doherty, an Irish immigrant who
wishes to return to His Majesty's dominions because he has been
told at the British consulate that all Irishmen who come to America die young of the fever.

The plot of the piece depends on another English traveler, John
Bull, a former suitor of Amelia whom she had told to sample the
world before proposing again. Still in love with her, he offers to
cure her brother of his prejudices if she will reward his success
with marriage. Disguised as an offensive Frenchman, he arranges
that they will all have passage together on a boat up the Hudson
River to Albany and from thence across the state to Niagara on
the Erie Canal. (A stationary steamboat was shown on stage,
while the scenery moved behind it.)

Bull carries out his plan in two disguises, as a Frenchman and
as a Yankee. His Frenchman is a parody of Wentworth as a traveler: he takes snuff and sneers; he is rude and then complains that
Wentworth is not civil to him. In one scene (*Act II, Scene 2*), Bull
parodies Wentworth directly; when Wentworth demands a
candle, the Frenchman demands two candles; when Wentworth
finally demands to be shown to bed, the Frenchman demands two
beds. The parody gives Wentworth a view of himself as seen by
others. Because it is a parody, the Frenchman still gets better service, thereby still more infuriating Wentworth. By a coincidence
admissible in a farce, Wentworth overhears Bull talking to his
razor while shaving. Thinking Bull is a Frenchman, he thinks the
razor that will serve for "John Bull" is meant for him as an Englishman; and he insists to his sister that there is a plot against his
life (*Act III, Scene 1*).

Bull makes his first appearance impersonating a Yankee at the
end of Act I, when he insists that the riverboat's piston is too
short. In the third and last act, the Yankee character is his chief
device. Telling Wentworth Yankee stories (wooden chestnuts and
so on), the Yankee character seems to Amelia to be reinforcing
Wentworth's prejudices rather than curing them. But by running
down his countrymen he gains Wentworth's favor. At the end of
the trip, Bull shakes Wentworth a bit by telling him he is right to
be angry at everyone laughing behind his back when "you have

such coaxing ways with you" (*Act III, Scene* 5). Bull plays on
Denis Doherty's fears with more and more outrageous stories,
finally accusing Americans of cannibalism. After snorting awhile,
Wentworth finally tells Bull, "Why would you encourage that
poor fellow's prejudices, when you know that neither the people
nor the country are as bad as you make them?" (*Act III, Scene* 5).
When Wentworth confesses that he has been unfair in his own
judgments and is actually civil to a waiter, Bull admits his mas-
querades; and Amelia admits her complicity. Since this is a Dunlap play, the suddenly good-natured Wentworth acquiesces to
their engagement.

The play is partly a gallery of stage types (Irish, Yankee,
French), but many of the minor characters complement the moving scenery, filling in the portrait of the land Wentworth rejects
and Amelia accepts. Coad complains about the play's "irrelevant
characters" (177); but, seen as part of the social landscape, they
serve a thematic function. A case in point is Dunlap's introduction
of James Fenimore Cooper's Leatherstocking into the play. Like
the other characters, part of his function is to display scenery,
leading Wentworth and Amelia to a scenic cataract in the Cats-
kills. In the last scene of the play he is posed picturesquely at
Niagara Falls. But he also serves more important functions. All
other native Americans in the play are of the servant class. If
Wentworth's final conversion is to be in the least believable, he
must meet an American whom he cannot disdain.

Leatherstocking is an appropriate agent for this purpose, for he
is not simply a popular literary figure to be used to garner applause; he is (and is still) an embodiment of one notion of the
ideal American. In the rough country around the cataract, Wentworth must rely on Leatherstocking's skill and prowess; even before forced to change his mind about America, he shows some
grudging admiration for Leatherstocking. Leatherstocking serves
two other functions as well: he provides a heroic American character for a play in which the principal hero is English, and he
personifies the natural beauty of America shown on the back-
drops. Amelia and her brother's different reactions to America are
partly the result of her willingness and his inability to appreciate
the beauty of nature; going up the Hudson River, she watches the
scenery, and he reads a paper. Wentworth misses in America the

luxuries of a sophisticated urban civilization. Leatherstocking speaks for those who resent the encroachments of civilization on nature.

One of the most interesting of the minor characters plays no real part in the plot—Job Jerryson, the Negro waiter at the New York hotel. He may be the first picture on the American stage of a realistic, well-educated, free Negro. He speaks with no trace of dialect but with a careful dignity: asked to accompany Amelia and Wentworth on their trip, he says, "I do not think I can be spared from the hotel at this time" (Act I, Scene 1). This character is not an idealized slave speaking free verse. Jerryson is a free man; he is a waiter, but he calls no man "master." His careful speech has a realistic source. He is one of the managers of a colored theatrical group, the Shakespearian Club. This detail is probably based on such groups active in New York in the 1820's.[8] He is consistently shown as superior to the white servants in the play: to Amelia's maid, who calls her "mistress" (Act I, Scene 1); to Denis Doherty, who thinks Jerryson must have the "black fever" (Act I, Scene 2); to the raucous steamboat runners (Act I, Scene 2); and to Doherty again, when the Irishman has missed the boat to Albany and set out on the road to Boston by mistake (Act II, Scene 1). Doherty is a stage Irishman, and Bull deliberately plays his Frenchman and Yankee as such; but Jerryson is an independent creation, a product of Dunlap's hatred of slavery and of his sympathy for free Negroes.

Although the play is partly based on American resentment of the unfavorable accounts published by prominent foreign travelers like Mrs. Trollope and Captain Basil Hall, Dunlap treats this theme in his usual conciliatory fashion. His preface explains his intentions: "The plan of making the prejudiced traveller owe his cure to one of his own countrymen, prevents (or was so intended) any disagreeable nationalities, and serves the further purpose of giving the author an excuse for the imperfections of the French, or Yankee character, as the representative of both is an Englishman." The result is a play about objectionable English travelers in which both hero and heroine are English. Only the Irish have reason to feel themselves unfairly depicted, and the unbelievably credulous Doherty is allowed to leave the country with the Wentworths. But Wentworth does promise to settle Doherty on a farm, and it is with him in mind that Wentworth speaks Dunlap's moral for the play: "When the film of prejudice is removed from his eye, man sees in his fellow man of every clime a brother" (*Act V, Scene 6*).

If we compare this last play with Dunlap's first play, *The Father*, it seems clear that Dunlap's long years in the theater brought a few advances in craftsmanship. *A Trip to Niagara* has a single plot, which is worked out well within the limits of probability allowed to farces. The romantic hero appears on stage from the beginning and is an active agent in the plot; neither is really the case in the earlier play. The heroine, Amelia, is neither as foolish as Mrs. Racket nor so maudlin as Caroline; and she is, accordingly, more attractive than either. As in *The Father*, minor characters like Leatherstocking and Jerryson are not tied directly to the action of the play, but they do support its theme; Jerryson and Leatherstocking emphasize positive aspects of the American scene, and Denis Doherty provides a lower-class mirror of Wentworth's prejudices. The moving scenery is likewise functional; it was certainly effective and surely as legitimate as the songs in Dunlap's "operas" (Caroline sings one song in *The Father*).

A Trip to Niagara seems less attractive today than, say, John Howard Payne's (and Washington Irving's) *Charles the Second* (1823), although Dunlap's play is at least as original. But *The Father* suffers in comparison with Tyler's *The Contrast*. *A Trip to Niagara* is well above average for its time. Not a great play, it is still the best of the surviving original comedies by Dunlap and by no means an unworthy end to his long career as a dramatist.

IV *The Lost Comedies*

Since Dunlap's sense of property was not overdeveloped, it is hard to say just how many of his unprinted plays were his own work and how many were revisions of English works under new titles. Two plays, *Forty and Twenty* and *Robespierre*, he lists as his but makes no comment about; they seem never to have been produced. *Forty and Twenty* is listed as a comedy, but it may or may not have been original. *Robespierre* is probably the same as the *Fall of Robespierre* which Dunlap once read aloud to the Friendly Club.[9] If so, it would be original and almost certainly a tragedy. The other unprinted original plays were comedies, and we can reconstruct something of their nature by examining Dunlap's and other comments on them.

The Miser's Wedding (1793) was played "in the hottest weather . . . without study or rehearsal. . . . The piece was murdered—it deserved death—and never heard of more" (Theatre, I, 198). Hodgkinson produced it against the wishes of Henry, who then refused the part intended for him. These few facts tell us little about the nature of the play, which is, however, described as a comedy; but they do confirm that Dunlap had not forgotten the lesson of The Modest Soldier and was now writing parts with specific actors in mind. That The Miser's Wedding was played at the instance of Hodgkinson indicates that Hodgkinson was Dunlap's contact with the company at this time.

More evidence for a relationship between Dunlap and Hodgkinson at this time is provided by the production of Shelty's Travels (1794), an interlude written for a Hodgkinson benefit at Hodgkinson's request. The actor had been a popular success in the comic role of Shelty in John O'Keeffe's The Highland Reel (1788). Dunlap's plot for this piece evidently told of Shelty leaving his native island for London, where he told his story to O'Keeffe; and later making his way to New York, where he saw various sights of the town. The play may also have contained the first stage reference to the difficulties of American shipping with the Algerian pirates.[10] Dunlap's task was obviously like that of writing Darby's Return for Wignell, and we may assume that he adopted a similar plan—the wide range of Shelty's travels makes it likely that Dunlap had Shelty narrate them, rather than crowd so many scenes into a short interlude. In the O'Keeffe play, Shelty is an innocent piper; the comedy of his travels no doubt arose from the naïveté of his observations on city life: like Jonathan in Tyler's The Contrast, Dunlap's Shelty visits a theater while in New York.

The Natural Daughter (1799) was played badly on a bad night; Dunlap's managership does not seem to have brought to his plays any more careful efforts by the actors. The title may be meant to recall Richard Cumberland's The Natural Son (1792), but the play itself sounds more or less original. Dunlap says it was "complicated and ineffective" (Theatre, II, 94), and what we know of the plot bears him out.[11] The natural daughter of Sir Stephen Sternford, deserted by her father, has been raised by his kind wife. When the wife dies, the daughter goes to London, where she learns of her birth. Sir Stephen's legitimate son, also deserted by his father, is posing as a footman in order to be near his beloved. Sir Stephen himself is courting another young girl, who recklessly marries him and then reforms him. Betrayed by false friends, Charles abandons his naïve romanticism and marries his beloved. The natural daughter's uncle and guardian ties together her story and the courtships of Charles and Sir Stephen. Charles is evidently another Dunlap son estranged from his father, while Sir Stephen is a stock type, the reformed rake. Since even Sir Stephen is both happy and moral at the end, *The Natural Daughter* fits easily into Dunlap's usual pattern.

The Temple of Independence (1799) was a short patriotic piece written for Washington's birthday. *The Soldier of '76* (1801) and *The Retrospect; or, The American Revolution* (1802) were also short pieces for patriotic occasions. A later play of which little is known, *The Battle of New Orleans* (1816), was probably another patriotic drama. Whether these should be classified as comedies we cannot say with any certainty, but Dunlap's extant patriotic plays, *Yankee Chronology* and *The Glory of Columbia*, mix comedy and patriotism and are laughable throughout.

A more substantial effort was an opera, *The Spanish Castle; or, The Knight of the Guadalquiver* (1800). A brief review said at the time that it was "received with that uncommon warmth of approbation which marks it as the popular piece of the season. The music is captivating." [12] The forecast was inaccurate, for it "was performed, not approved of, repeated once, and forgotten" (*Theatre*, II, 136); it lost money. Neither the review nor Dunlap tells much about its plot, but the castle may suggest a Gothic setting and the knight the robber plot used in *The Knight's Adventure*. We know somewhat more about *Bonaparte in England* (1803), which was based on a contemporary newspaper anecdote (Coad, p. 174). A German Jewish broker is mistaken by English authorities for Jerome Bonaparte; even more confused, an Irish officer thinks him to be the famous Napoleon. He does his best to live up to the description. This farce has a promising premise and was thought worthy enough to be revived as part of the program for the Dunlap benefit in 1833, but it was never printed.

The Proverb; or, Conceit Can Cure, Conceit Can Kill (1804) introduced to the American theater the traveling mountebank quack and his stage. Rightly or wrongly, the author attributes its thin audience to its "being known as American" (*Theatre,* II, 207). *Lewis of Monte Blanco; or, The Transplanted Irishman* (1804) was produced soon after *The Proverb* and was a success, perhaps because, following so closely on the other's heels, it "was not supposed to be the manager's" (*Theatre,* II, 208). Lewis, the villain, has kidnapped his brother Jerome and daughter, in hopes of marrying the girl and acquiring some property in Jerome's possession. The daughter, of course, is in love with a nice young man. Thady O'Reilly, the transplanted Irishman, blows up part of Lewis' castle and performs other good deeds. The prisoners are also aided by a servant who helps them escape and by a dotty female who wanders about convincing everyone she is a ghost. All ends happily, despite the Gothic setting of the castle.[13] The play resembles *Darby's Return* in that it was written for Harwood, who had already caught the public's fancy in Irish parts.

Of these lost plays, we may wish that one or two survived to show us more of Dunlap's work in comedy—*Bonaparte in England* certainly, and perhaps *The Proverb* or *Lewis of Monte Blanco.* For the most of the other lost plays, Dunlap himself has little good to say; and we are in no position to revise his judgment. What we can learn of the plots and aims of these plays indicates that most were written to order, most were derivative, and most were either patriotic pageants or sentimental comedies. The comedies which have survived show neither great wit nor unusual ingenuity. The best of them provide competent pieces of theater; they allow actors opportunities to please the audience with new variations on stock roles.

CHAPTER 4

Tragedy and Melodrama

D UNLAP'S most serious efforts can be distinguished from his comedies by the presence of an occasional death, by the use of blank verse, and by the absence of intentional humor. The world in which they take place is the same as that of the comedies. *Leicester* is a romantic tragedy; *André*, a historical drama; both *Ribbemont* and *Man of Fortitude*, Gothic plays. But all four are also sentimental dramas because they are built around sentimental situations and because they affirm the essential goodness of man. The only real villains in these plays are off-stage ones; on stage, ignorance and misunderstanding take the place of evil. Dunlap could admire an Iago, but he could not create one. The world of these plays knows friendship or ill-will, fortune or misfortune; but it has no heights or depths of feeling, although the characters call upon God or the Devil. At least two of these plays, *Leicester* and *André*, are among Dunlap's best; but they are successful only on their own terms.

I Leicester

Leicester was first played in 1794 under the title of *The Fatal Deception; or, The Progress of Guilt*, although *Leicester* was apparently its working title from the beginning. Dunlap believed it was "the first American tragedy that was performed by professed players" (*Theatre*, I, 218), a significance probably more properly awarded to Thomas Godfrey's *Prince of Partia* (1767). Dunlap, who knew of Godfrey's play, thought it had never been performed. Dunlap's own tragedy does mark the real beginning of native tragedy on the stage; his plays were to prompt others to write, as Tyler's comedy had prompted him. As Dunlap's first tragedy, *Leicester* has some interest, independent of its merits. The date of its writing is unclear. The published edition (1807) says that it was first written in 1790, but Dunlap later wrote that it was "finished" about December, 1793.[1] Perhaps the version Hodgkinson read aloud to a literary group in 1793 was a revision of an earlier, complete draft. It was Hodgkinson, too, who produced the play, on the same benefit bill with *Shelty's Travels*.

The plot of *Leicester* is complicated, but its various strands are well integrated and converge at the play's end. The first act is spent largely in exposition that is more skillfully handled than in *The Father*. Each fact we learn hints at more than we are told. Edred, a faithful servant, tells Leicester's friend Howard to dissuade Leicester from returning to Kenilworth; but he does not tell us why. Leicester tells Howard that he is anxious to return. Once he had slighted Matilda, but he fell in love with her when she came to London as the wife of Essex; and he has secretly married her after she has become a widow. He and Howard save Dudley Cecil and Elwina from robbers, and he insists that they spend the night at Kenilworth. Coming home unexpectedly *and* bringing guests, Leicester is obviously a ripe subject for tragedy. Dudley and Elwina are in guilty flight of some sort, one which has already driven Elwina half mad. We learn soon that part of Dudley's burden of guilt is having intrigued against his younger brother Henry, persuading their older brother, Lord Cecil, to send Henry away. At the very end of the act, Elwina urges Dudley to confess to Leicester that he has killed Lord Cecil.

The opening of the second act makes clear what Edred was hinting at: Henry Cecil has been living in adultery with Matilda. Hopelessly in love with her, he is nevertheless remorseful, for he reveres Leicester. Matilda is convinced that Leicester must die for their happiness. She has never forgiven him for slighting her before she was the wife of the great Essex. Henry has almost persuaded her to run away with him instead of murdering Leicester, but Leicester returns too soon. Matilda introduces Henry as her brother. When word arrives that her real brother is on his way to Kenilworth, Matilda urges the guilt-ridden Henry to kill her husband. Henry agrees to do it for her sake: "I will. I am resolved. Hell, I'm thine own./Come, all ye demons, who delight in man's/ Damnation, hover smiling round the scene!/And when my heart shall whisper, 'Lei'ster loves thee,'/Answer, 'Or Lei'ster or Matilda dies'" (*Act II, Scene 2*).

In the third act, which has an unusual amount of action for a

Dunlap play, Henry mopes about, while Matilda urges that the deed be done quickly so the blame can be put on the unidentified strangers (Dudley and Elwina). Dudley tells Leicester his story, more interesting to the audience because only partly revealed in the first two acts. Dudley had found his older brother leaving Matilda's home and had killed him in a jealous fit, learning only too late that his brother had only called to learn what sort of woman Dudley was going to marry. Dudley asks Leicester to look out for Henry if he finds him and goes off to bed in Leicester's room. Still shrinking from his task, Henry persuades Matilda to draw the curtains from outside so that he will not have to look on Leicester's face as he kills him. Dudley's voice comes from within, tossing in his sleep and begging forgiveness; but Henry thinks he is hearing spirits. He rushes in and kills his brother, thinking him Leicester, although he is shaken by his victim crying "Cecil" as he dies.

Dunlap returns to his normal playwriting habits in the fourth act, which is devoted to the characters' discovering what the audience knows anyway. Howard and Edred finally get around to telling Leicester of Matilda's infidelity. Henry is shocked to find Leicester alive, decides he is glad, and then discovers he killed his own brother. When Elwina comes in, she goes mad; she seems to think she killed Dudley. But Leicester, observing the odd behavior of his supposed brother-in-law and finding a corpse in his bedroom, has come to suspect that Howard and Edred may be right in their suspicions.

In the fifth act, Howard and Edred tell Leicester that Matilda has been seen brewing poison for him; and they propose to turn the tables on her. Leicester is reluctant, but they point out that he is in a precarious position. Matilda tries to talk things over with Henry, but he has used all his courage murdering Dudley and has no time for anything but remorse. In the banquet hall, Matilda offers Leicester some home-cooked food; but Howard and Edred enter and accuse her of her crimes. She retires in momentary confusion, and they switch the plates. Calming herself, she returns to suggest they continue eating; but Leicester will not let her take the poisoned plate. Having been found out, she stabs herself and dies. Assassins enter; but Henry arrives, armed, and tells them to leave Leicester for him. Leicester throws back his cloak and reveals that he is armored and armed. While Howard and Edred drive off the assassins, Henry forces Leicester to a duel. Henry then drops his own sword and runs upon Leicester's. He confesses his name and guilt. Leicester forgives him, expressing the charitable hope that heaven will do the same.

In prefatory remarks to the printed version, Dunlap says that "To most readers, Matilda urging Henry to the murder of Leicester will appear as a copy of Lady Macbeth; but she is, in reality, more in situation like the Clytemnestra of the Greek poets: yet essentially different (independent of differences in merit) from both." The modesty of the parenthetical remark is typical of Dunlap—as is the touch of disingenuousness in dealing with a literary debt. The situation is indeed like Clytemnestra, but the debt to *Macbeth* is more specific. Leicester is to be killed as Duncan is killed, and the scene in which Matilda drives the hesitant Henry to the deed attempts to capture the effect of its parallel in *Macbeth*. The next day Henry sees what he first thinks is a ghost.[2] Although *Leicester* is one of Dunlap's more original plays, it is not wholly original.

Macbeth's opportunity to kill Duncan is in part an accident of fate, but his motive for doing so is not, and the rest of his misdeeds follow from his first. In contrast, the plot of *Leicester* depends upon a series of accidents: that Leicester should rescue Dudley and Elwina on his way home and bring them to his castle; that he arrives just before Henry and Matilda run away together; that Henry and Dudley never see each other, although it is understandable that Henry should avoid the company once Leicester arrives home: managing this requires that Leicester enter first alone, that Henry then retire, and that Dudley and Elwina be brought in only after he leaves. It is also accidental that Matilda's real brother should be on his way to visit, preventing her and Henry from planning an effective flight. Getting Dudley into the room and making it pitch dark are managed by the playwright but at some expense of probability. Elwina's madness is prefigured but very convenient. Some of these coincidences and improbabilities are mere theatrical conventions, but Leicester's inopportune arrival and his hospitality to Dudley and Elwina are basic to the plot; their accidental nature thus affects the seriousness of the play as a whole.

Dunlap's prologue (never played) does assert serious intentions. It insists again on the morality of the drama—the tragic muse's intent is "in Virtue's ways to fix the mind." After observing that England will never see another Shakespeare and that the muse now seems to reside in Germany (with Schiller), Dunlap hopes that the muse will take up her work in America. But, though Leicester says that the tragedy shows the effects of "Guilty Pleasure" (*Act V, Scene 3*), the play is not in fact didactic. We may also say that writing a tragedy about Elizabethan England is an odd way to establish the tragic muse in America.

Macbeth murders for power; Henry Cecil, for love. Yet *Leicester* is not about love, adultery, or even "Guilty Pleasure." The adulterous love between Henry and Matilda is simply a necessary premise; they have no time for romantic dalliance in the play itself. If the play is about anything, it is about guilt and remorse. The theme is introduced in the first act with Dudley and Elwina. Elwina says guilt "is a whirlpool, drawing heedless mortals/Near and more near—then, plunging them to death" (*Act I*).

This theme may be connected with the father-son conflicts found in other Dunlap plays. The guilt is felt first toward father figures, the slain elder brother, the threatened Leicester. Henry knew Matilda before her marriage, but there are still Oedipal overtones in the situation; after all, it is in his bedroom that Leicester is to be murdered. Consider, too, the phallic implications of the last scene: Leicester and Henry hold their swords out before them; Henry signals his guilt about his sin against Leicester's manhood by dropping his sword and rushing upon Leicester's.

Even if we reject this line of analysis, guilt remains Henry's chief characteristic—guilt for his adultery, guilt for his murder—and Henry is the play's real protagonist, the part Hodgkinson took for himself. Leicester exists as an object of Henry's guilt and finally as his executioner and father confessor. What is made to matter in the play's central scene is not whether Leicester is killed but whether or not Henry will damn himself by killing him. Dudley is Henry's brother in more than one way, for he mirrors his guilt; like Henry at the end, Dudley has little wish to live left to him and is only kept going by concern for one he loves. The chief female character, Matilda, does not share Henry's remorse. If she did, the play could hardly proceed; their liaison would be discovered. And, in any case, the audience could not bear a second character as guiltily long-winded as Henry.

Henry's long disquisitions about his remorse are a part of the play's link with sentimental comedy—the exploitation of emotions for their own sake. Another link is the final absolution which Leicester offers Henry: he does not offer forgiveness because he has come to understand Henry's suffering—he has not had opportunity to do so—but because he is, despite his grim surroundings, much the same all-forgiving character as Colonel Duncan in *The Father*, who easily forgives Ranter for making him believe his son was dead. Leicester might offer forgiveness because he recognizes that it was his snobbish slight which led Matilda to seek drastic revenge, but he does not remember this factor. It is, in fact, hard to reconcile that earlier Leicester with the man in the play, who has become a stock character—a benevolent, heroic older man.

Leicester has tolerable blank verse, adequate construction, thematic unity, and several well-realized characters (not including Leicester himself). But although it ends with three major characters dead and one mad, it lacks moral seriousness. It does not exist in a tragic universe; instead, it has one foot in our own world, in which people committing sins and crimes sometimes have bad luck, and one foot in a purely theatrical world, in which characters speak in blank verse and prefer death to dishonor. The verse rises higher than the plot allows the characters to do. The play is not art but entertainment; as such, it is one of Dunlap's two or three best plays.

II   Ribbemont

In the fall of 1796, Dunlap brought out *The Mysterious Monk*, the first of his own plays produced under his own managership. A revised version was produced in 1803 under the title of *Ribbemont; or, The Feudal Baron*, under which title it was later printed. When it was revived, a reviewer remarked that it had earlier been "laid on the shelf after the second performance—we hope it will resume its station." [3] Dunlap, who agrees that it was "not skillfully managed," says "The characters and incidents were not in sufficient number" (*Theatre*, I, 299, 300–301). It seeks to appeal to the public's liking for the Gothic: the scenes include an ancient castle and a Gothic chapel complete with tomb; the plot includes deaths that are not deaths, threats never carried out, and resurrections that are purely natural.[4]

The first act of *Ribbemont* resembles that of *Leicester* in depending on incomplete exposition for its effectiveness. Ribbemont's young son Theodore, who returns home to mourn for his dead mother, finds his father deep in excessive grief. Manuel, the mysterious monk, warns him not to believe his father if he speaks ill of the dead Countess. Theodore is angry at any suggestion that anyone might speak ill of his mother or that his father might tell an untruth. But, when he persists in praising the Countess to Ribbemont, the baron tells him that he murdered her. Ribbemont had received letters hinting that his wife was sleeping with his friend Narbonne. Her maid admitted having seen a man visit the Countess's chambers nightly. Ribbemont lay in wait, but the villain escaped. Ribbemont then rode to Narbonne's, insisted on a duel, and left him dying. Procuring some poison from a monastery, he went home and poisoned his wife. Having had doubts about the guilt of the dead planted by Manuel, Theodore points out that neither Narbonne nor the Countess was accused or had confessed; the thought has not occurred to Ribbemont, and it disturbs him.

In the next act, Theodore goes to the chapel to ask Manuel how he knows the Countess was innocent. The Countess, who had been given a sleeping potion instead of poison, is hiding in the tomb and sighs to hear her son's voice. Manuel tells Theodore he is disturbing her sleeping spirit and steers him away. Soon Ribbemont receives a letter from a disgruntled peasant whom he had insulted and kept from marrying the Countess's maid. The maid and her lover have fooled Ribbemont into suspecting his wife and his friend and have fled together. Theodore sets off in pursuit, while Ribbemont shuts himself in his room to savor his remorse. Manuel, who tricks his way inside the castle, leads Ribbemont to express his remorse over killing Narbonne. When Manuel seems on the verge of telling Ribbemont that the Countess lives, word comes that Theodore has found and killed the fleeing pair and is soon to be hanged for it.

The last two acts devote much time on arguments between Ribbemont and Theodore over who should die and how. Theodore, like André later, does not wish to die by hanging and asks his father to bring him poison, so he can die a more respectable death in his cell. Ribbemont wants to die with him, but Theodore says that would make his own death an obvious suicide. When Ribbemont returns with the poison, he renews his vow to take it with his son. Rather than die a "cowardly suicide" (*Act V, Scene 1*), or obviously one, Theodore now swears he will die on the gibbet.

When Ribbemont prepares to take the poison, Theodore takes it away; and the father then draws his sword to kill himself. Theodore begs him not to and starts to take the poison so that he may make this plea his dying request. Ribbemont stops him. The reader begins to wish they would both take it, and audiences must have felt the same.

Fortunately, the Countess, who sped away to the judges at the end of the fourth act, enters now at the end of the fifth with a pardon for Theodore. Her son had forbidden his father to disclose the whole story—the family name was at stake—but the Countess, whose "murder" was the worst of it, has told all and won the judge's pity. Her husband is at first too shocked and guilt-ridden to receive her, but when she insists that she forgives him, they embrace. When Ribbemont laments that he is still guilty of Narbonne's murder, Manuel reveals that he is Narbonne. Saved by the monks, he has been working to bring about this happy final curtain.

A good portion of the story is already over when the curtain first rises, for *Ribbemont* is a play of big speeches and big scenes in which little really happens. The most striking action, the murder of the fleeing servants, takes place off stage, and Theodore tells his father he had not meant to do it. No one on stage regrets these deaths much, and the audience is not meant to and probably cannot since the two slain characters have never been on stage. The big scenes of the play are made possible by the characters' ignorance of the true state of affairs: that the Countess and Narbonne live; that Theodore is not irrevocably doomed to die. If Narbonne-Manuel were not so devious in his efforts to right matters, the last three acts would be actionless—a point the Countess makes to him when she first learns of Theodore's plight.

If we accept Narbonne's belief that he and the Countess should be thoroughly cleared before revealing themselves, then the play is relatively free of the reliance on coincidence found in *Leicester*. The Countess's opportune arrival in the final scene is acceptable in terms of stage convention. The revelation that Manuel is Narbonne in disguise is well anticipated. His special knowledge and his interest in Ribbemont's remorse over Narbonne's death both serve as clues. When he agrees to accompany the Countess to the judges, his tone is so martial that the Countess says, "That burst spoke more the soldier than the monk" (*Act IV, Scene 2*). The original title, *The Mysterious Monk*, may have made his identity all too clear.

The most important theme of *Ribbemont* is false pride and overconcern with honor, and the play's moral is that men would be better off with less honor and more humility. Both Ribbemont and Theodore must learn this fact. Ribbemont's false pride in his position led him to mistreat his vassal and then to mistrust his wife. His false sense of honor made him strike at Narbonne and the Countess without asking questions. "Nought was in malice done," he assures Theodore, "but all in honor" (*Act I, Scene 2*). At the beginning of the play, Theodore also believes that whatever the church may say

> the lofty baron,
> The pillar of the state, his king's support,
> And master of the life or death of thousands;
> Must not let e'en the safety of his soul
> Be put in competition with his honor.
> (*Act I, Scene 4*)

Narbonne-Manuel is the chief teacher of the play's lesson. In the end, Ribbemont proves an apt pupil. When Theodore tells him that suicide would be dishonorable, Ribbemont replies, "Honor is not the idol it was once" (*Act IV, Scene 1*). And Ribbemont is able to sum up the honor theme in a final curtain speech in praise of Narbonne:

> For, what was lost thro' honor, falsely nam'd
> . . . .
> Has he thro' pure benevolence restored;
> And won my soul to reason and to virtue.
> (*Act V*)

This speech points to the connection of the play with the world of "pure benevolence" in sentimental comedy. It is to "reason," as well as benevolence, that the baron has been won; for the world of tender and benevolent sentiments is also a world ruled by a Deistic God who has planted a natural morality in man. So long as one holds fast to reason, he is bound to act rightly. The false monk points out to Ribbemont that it was his *"passions"* which played him false (*Act III, Scene 3*). Had the baron shown benevolence,

his vassal would not have devised a plot against him. Had Ribbemont been reasonable, the plot would never have succeeded. The
worship of one's own honor is thus wrong because it interferes
with benevolence toward others and with reason's check upon
one's actions.

Honor is the theme, but the plot is that of a domestic melodrama—family misunderstandings are resolved at the last minute.
Once again, we have a father and son estranged, this time because
the father has murdered the mother. The fleeing vassals have
plotted against Ribbemont because of his coldness and because he
will not let them wed. These might be seen today as double dis-
tortions of the father in the Oedipal triangle, who stands between
the child and its mother. The rebellious lovers are thus mirrors of
Theodore's own desires, and for that reason he must pursue and
kill them. But it is not enough to repress these desires, for he is
guilty of having felt them. So the focus of the play shifts to Theodore, who is condemned to die and is only saved by the interces-
sion of his mother. Behind the long scene in which Theodore and
Ribbemont discuss which is more anxious to die is a father-son
rivalry and repressed desire for the other's death. It is also of interest that the plot is initiated when Ribbemont strikes down his
wife's "innocent" lover, Narbonne. As usual, Dunlap ends with
innocence, guilt, remorse, forgiveness, and reconciliation.

Too much of the action takes place or has already taken place
off stage for the plot to grip the audience. Much depends on sentiments; but Ribbemont's remorse is less well expressed than
Henry's in *Leicester,* and of less intrinsic interest, since his actions
have been less consequential than he believes. Only Manuel does
more than react to events, and his motives and character are never
made clear. Instead, they are deliberately concealed from the audience in order to use his unmasking as a final stage coup. Dunlap's comment that there were too few characters might well be
amended to say that there is too little characterization, only good
acting parts. The blank verse, although rarely as overwrought as
some of that in *Leicester,* is also less eloquent. The play as a
whole cannot be considered a step forward.

III *Dunlap or Hodgkinson?*

The Man of Fortitude; or, The Knight's Adventure (1797) was published as by Hodgkinson, and the question of its authorship is in many ways more interesting than the play itself.[5] Whether Dunlap or Hodgkinson be the author, the play is derivative, meretricious entertainment. One source of the plot is probably Godwin's *Caleb Williams,* a novel whose hero finds himself in a ruined castle thought haunted by the local peasantry but actually used as a hideout by a band of robbers. More generally, the drama takes its place within a large group of "robber" plays initiated by the international success of Schiller's *Die Räuber* (1781). Dunlap's friend Smith had used the motif in an opera, *Edwin and Angelina,* which Dunlap had produced unsuccessfully in 1796.

As published, the drama is a Gothic drama in the first act and a robber play in the second. When the action opens on a gloomy heath in the midst of a storm, Sir Bertrand is on his way to ransom the king of France from Emperor Charles; but he must take refuge from the storm. His servant Carlos is frightened and regrets the three years they have spent at the wars. Sir Bertrand reproaches him for reminding him of the event which first set them wandering—the abduction of his bride on his wedding night by the villain Biron. There is a castle near, and they determine to take refuge in it, although a passing peasant tells them it is haunted. As they stand outside a gloomy castle lit by lightning, blue lights flash in the windows, and the door creaks open to receive them. Sir Bertrand insists on entering. Inside are a winding staircase, more blue lights, and a song by a female voice which reminds Sir Bertrand again of his lost Hortensia. A bloody specter beckons for the knight to follow him; convinced "thou art mortal" (*Act I, Scene 3*), the knight does so. Tired of being led about the castle, he finally draws his sword on the specter; and they both disappear through a trap door in the floor. Back in front of the winding staircase, three ghosts in Furies' masks carry off Carlos.

The second act takes place in the underground cavern where the robbers are hidden. The specter was their Captain, who tells Sir Bertrand he must die for finding their hiding place. The other bandits want the sentence carried out immediately. Our hero explains his mission and promises not to reveal their secrets, and the

Captain promises to think matters over. The Captain and knight depart, and the other bandits bring in Carlos with the hope of learning something to persuade their Captain to dispose of Sir Bertrand. But, when told Sir Bertrand is dead, Carlos swears they might as well kill him too since the best of masters is dead. The Captain confides to Sir Bertrand that he has for three years held a female prisoner, who has refused his honorable suit. To purchase his freedom, Sir Bertrand agrees to speak to her on the Captain's behalf—and, of course, the lovesick Captain's prisoner is his Hortensia. The bandits had intercepted Biron, killed him, and kidnapped her.

The Captain, returning to find them together, feels betrayed. He has his men take Bertrand away and tells Hortensia that she must yield to him now or he will take her by force. She grabs the dagger from his belt and threatens him with it, while insisting that he is a coward to attack a defenseless woman. He retreats in understandable confusion. Down in the torture room, Sir Bertrand is stretched on the rack. The Captain points out that he has had three years to adjust to losing Hortensia and would now lose nothing by renouncing her again, but the hero will not do so. Hortensia is brought in to observe matters. When calling on Heaven to strike the villain dead brings no results, she agrees to yield to the Captain if he frees Sir Bertrand, who strongly advises against the bargain. He is released; but, when the Captain goes to Hortensia, she makes an unsuccessful attempt to stab him.

The Captain is unaccountably so impressed with her devotion and heroism that he forgives her her trickery. When he asks his men to do likewise, "*all the* banditti *throw down their swords and cry*" (*Act II, Scene 4*)—a stage direction that seems to look forward to Gilbert and Sullivan's *Pirates of Penzance*, the ultimate robber play, although it evidently refers to the bandits' shouts of "Pardon! Pardon!" The Captain reveals the injustice which, of course, has led him to his life of crime; he was driven off his land after stopping a nobleman from raping his sister. The nobleman, it seems, was Biron, the bride-stealer. Carlos is brought in and freed; Sir Bertrand vows to have the Captain pardoned; and the curtain is brought down on a scene of disgusting sentimentality.

As Dunlap relates the creation of this play, he wrote a blank-verse one-act, *The Knight's Adventure*, and left it with Hodgkinson. Sometime later, Hodgkinson produced *The Man of Fortitude* as his own. When Dunlap observed that it was simply his play with some additions, Hodgkinson said only that he had "altered everything" (*Theatre*, I, 330). Dunlap did not get his own play back for some time after Hodgkinson's was produced. Dunlap included the play in his prospectus for the proposed ten-volume edition of his plays, but it was among those not published; we may hope, however, that he intended to publish his original play since no one could wish to take responsibility for the play as we have it. The incident may have caused ill-feeling at the time, but Dunlap later took a forgiving attitude: "We scarcely believe the author was conscious of wrong in the transaction, as far as injury to another was concerned" (*Theatre*, I, 330).

Even so, Dunlap's account of the affair may not be wholly just. He implies that Hodgkinson's alterations were minor, but the "comic buffoon, and a lady" (*Theatre*, I, 330) can only be Carlos and Hortensia. In the play as we have it, the plot of the second act turns on Hortensia, and Carlos provides what interest the first act holds, apart from scenic effects. It is possible Dunlap made somewhat more of the social injustices supposed to motivate the Captain and his bandits; but doing so would be in the tradition of the robber play. Hodgkinson probably took from Dunlap the basic notion and some dialogue, but his play is not much less original than some of Dunlap's adaptations. What he made of Dunlap's play cannot have added to Dunlap's pride as an author, but the piece seems to have been slight enough to begin with.

IV André *and Its Revision*

As a boy in New York City, Dunlap must have heard much about the virtues and fate of Major André, the young British officer sent on a mission to Benedict Arnold, caught, and hanged as a spy. According to Dunlap's preface to the printed version, he began work on *André* (1798) "More than nine years" before its eventual completion and production.[6] "Many circumstances" prevented his finishing it—his marriage must have been among them. Dunlap mentions in particular "a prevailing opinion that recent events are unfit subjects for tragedy" (p. iii). He saw his play as the test of this proposition. But, if the play failed, "the question must remain undetermined until some more powerful writer shall again make the experiment" (p. vi). The question was to remain open; *André* has come to be thought of as Dunlap's best play, but it was a failure in performance.

The action of *André* is simple. André is to be executed; and he is, despite a succession of attempts to save him. All acknowledge that André is an attractive and basically virtuous young man; all admit that the normal fate of a spy is to be hanged, and that this fate is just. The man of reason, M'Donald, will not see anything but justice in André's death. The man of feeling, Bland, sees only the horror of a good man's dying. Between these two are André, who has mastered himself enough to see the justice of his own death, and the General (obviously Washington), who admires André even while condemning him to die. The dramatic tensions thus reflect the real moral dilemma posed by André's situation.

The first act introduces the separate elements of this tension. Bland, returning from the South, is at first glad to hear that Arnold's British co-conspirator has been captured and is to die; but he is shocked to hear the prisoner is André. When Bland was a prisoner, André not only saved him and others from the horrors of a prison ship but personally nursed Bland back to health before his exchange. Bland cannot believe him guilty and vows to save him. At the encampment, M'Donald will not agree with Seward that André deserves pity; he has been "sunk by misdeed, not fortune" (*Act I, Scene 2*). But the General gives equal justice to the claims of righteousness and mercy:

> Worthy M'Donald, though it suits full well
> The virtuous man to frown on all misdeeds,
> Yet ever keep in mind that man is frail;
>
> . . . .
>
> Sure it is not Virtues voice that triumphs
> In his ruin.
>
> (*Act I, Scene 2*)

The second act prepares for the efforts to save André. Bland goes to his cell, where André is giving thanks that he failed to win the hand of his beloved Honora since she is thus spared his shame. Bland insists that André was only doing his duty and is virtuous still, but his friend André will not accept these excuses for himself: he acted against his own reason and conscience and is prepared to die. Bland swears that if he dies

I will forswear my country and her service;
I'll hie me to the Briton, and with fire,
And sword, and every instrument of death
Or devastation, join in the work of war!
What, shall worth weigh for nought? I will avenge thee!
(*Act II, Scene 1*)

But André does not wish to "cause another traitor" and absolves the Americans of guilt in his death. Bland goes to plead with the General. Meanwhile, Bland's mother and family learn that Bland's father, now a British prisoner, will be killed in retaliation if André is executed.

The General explains to Bland that he must condemn the admirable André, lest clemency encourage treason or allow the British to misjudge the Americans' ability to enforce the laws of war. Bland is so enraged that he rips the cockade from his helmet and stomps out. Since no one else is present, the General feels he can forgive Bland's rashness because his motives are pure. Hearing of his father's danger, Bland urges his mother to plead with the General. A British officer arrives first with a threatening note from Clinton, the British commander. Another note arrives from Bland's father, telling the General to ignore their friendship and do his duty. Hearing of this development, André sends the same messenger back with his last request: that Bland's father be spared.

Enraged by M'Donald's rational insistence that André must die, Bland tries to provoke him into a duel but cannot, and rushes out to brand M'Donald as a coward. Mrs. Bland tells M'Donald that her pleas have been in vain. Bland, recognizing that he has behaved like "The weather-cock of passion! fool inebriate" (*Act IV, Scene 2*), visits André, who gives him a letter and some tokens to give to Honora. But Honora's father, opposed to his suit, had deceived André. She, who loved him truly and wed no other, now arrives just as the guards come to take him to be executed. They kindly agree to give Honora time to plead with the General.

Bland now apologizes to M'Donald, who forgives him. In lines added to appease audiences offended on the first night by Bland's relinquishing his cockade and the service of his country, M'Donald gives Bland the cockade that has been given to him by the General for safe-keeping. The General is moved by Honora's sorrow, but word comes that the British have hanged an American scout. "Why, why, my country, did I hesitate!" says the General. André, who can read his fate in Bland's countenance, prepares to die bravely. Honora makes his doing so more difficult by showing up and going mad as he is led away. A short scene shows him crossing the stage in intelligent conversation with his guards on his way to be hanged. M'Donald hurries Bland away as a cannon signals André's end.

The influence of Thomas Otway's popular *Venice Preserved: or, a Plot Discovered* has been discerned in the last act of *André*.[7] Bland refers to it in his last scene with his friend:

> I do remember
> When a boy at school, in our allotted tasks,
> We, by our puny acts, strove to portray
> The giant thoughts of Otway. I was Pierre—
> O, thou are Pierre's reality! a soldier,
> On whose manly brow sits fortitude enamor'd;
> A Mars, abhorring vice, yet doomed to die
> A death of infamy; thy corse expos'd
> To vulgar gaze—halter'd—distorted—Oh!!
> Pierre had a friend to save him from such shame—
> And so hast thou.
>
> (*Act V, Scene 3*)

Doomed to hang as a conspirator, Pierre, like André, is a hero; Jaffeir, who has betrayed his friend, is, like Bland, implicated in his death. But, despite Bland's tactful description of his approaching fate, André thinks suicide a coward's way out and bids Bland live unmarked by murder to care for Honora.

Venice Preserved (with Forrest and Kemble) was the major attraction at the testimonial benefit for Dunlap in 1833. It was a good showcase for any company with two strong male leads, and Dunlap may have been encouraged to bring his own play forward by the strong playing of Cooper and Hodgkinson in the Otway play in Cooper's first appearance with the New York company. André (Hodgkinson) and Bland (Cooper) should have provided ample scope for their talents, but Cooper did not do his best for his new manager:

Young Bland was not the hero of the piece, and very little of the author's blank verse came *un-amended* from the mouth of the tragedian. In what was intended as the most pathetic scene of the play, between Cooper and Hodgkinson, the first, as Bland, after repeating, "Oh André—oh, André," as often as "Jemmy Thomson" wrote "Oh, Sophonisba," approached the unfortunate André, who in vain waited for *his* cue, and, falling in a burst of sorrow on his neck, cried, loud enough to be heard at the side scene, "Oh, André—damn the prompter!—Oh, André! What's next, Hodgkinson?" and sunk in unutterable sorrow on the breast of his overwhelmed friend, upon whose more practised stage cleverness he relied for support in the trying scene—*trying* to the author as well as actor and audience.

(*Theatre*, II, 21–22)

Whatever the outside influences, Dunlap demonstrated in other plays an interest in the situations and emotions found in *André*. The hero's situation is like that of Theodore in the prison scenes of *Ribbemont*, and similar personal roots seem indicated. Bland rebels against the father figure of the General, and he is less stirred by the possible death of his father than that of his friend. Bland insists André is innocent; André accepts his guilt and punishment. Together they act out the hostility to the father and the denial and guilt that may be associated with it. The end, of course, is reconciliation.

We almost need obscure personal motives to explain Dunlap's notion that the first American tragedy on a native subject should have a British spy for a hero. Cooper's fondness for the part was not increased by the violent audience reaction to Bland's throwing down his cockade. The black cockade was soon to be a Federalist party symbol (Quinn, p. 86n.). Dunlap's preface says the audience eruption was caused by offended "veterans" (p. v). This seems more likely than any purely partisan interpretation of the affair, although the play is sometimes said to present a "Federalist point of view" (Quinn, p. 88). Dunlap was aware that "The subject necessarily involves political questions" (p. iii), and his prologue asks the audience to let "no party spirit" determine its response.

The great political question in the play is the nature of America's relationship with Europe, which is discussed at some length

in a scene between M'Donald and Seward (*Act II, Scene 2*).
M'Donald sees the Atlantic as a link between "Columbia's shores"
and those of Europe. Seward would rather see barriers "impas-
sible to man" in the ocean's place, so that here might arise a society "free from the extremes of poverty and riches" and from Europe's vices. He fears peace will bring a horde of Europeans to
America to infect it with ills.[8] M'Donald is more optimistic:

> From Europe shall enriching commerce flow,
> And many an ill attendent; but from thence
> Shall likewise flow blest Science. Europe's knowledge
> By sharp experience bought, we should appropriate.

Here the terms of reference are cultural, and refer to Europe as a
whole—to the France admired by the Jeffersonians as well as to
the England still admired by Federalists. In the final curtain
speech, M'Donald hopes that America's children will be taught
not only about the Revolution but also about judging the English
by "their proper, individual deeds" (*Act V, Scene 5*).

M'Donald's speech points to the essential moral of the English
relationship as seen in the play. However virtuous he is, it is right
that André should die. The Revolution is a just cause. Off stage,
the English behave like villains, threatening the life of Bland's
father, illegally hanging an American scout. But (unlike *Yankee
Chronology*) this play does not suggest that the English are eter-
nally guilty. In its day, this viewpoint would fall more sympathetically on Federalist than on Jeffersonian ears. In the perspective of
history, it seems little more than Dunlap's normal good sense and
love of reconciliation. Certainly, it was the only view a dramatist
so indebted to English models could fairly adopt.

M'Donald is open to all of Europe, and it is not policy he hopes
to acquire from it but knowledge. Seward is the one who expresses the dream of an isolated America—which recalls Washington's Farewell Address, as sometimes interpreted—and
M'Donald displays the rationalism associated with Jeffersonianism
and is accused by Seward of "Mere theoretic dreaming" (*Act II,
Scene 2*). *André* is not a political tract but a play which touches
on the permanent problem of America's relationship with European civilization, a problem pressing for her first artists and intellectuals but no less pressing for a Henry James or a T. S. Eliot.

But M'Donald is not the hero but André. Hodgkinson took the part, but Cooper may have been wrong to think Bland an inferior role, for André's is almost wholly passive. Yet it is a good role, one which permits the actor to declaim any number of uplifting sentiments. Although Dunlap publishes the records of André's confinement with the 1798 edition of the play, he does not allow his André to shift the blame on Arnold, as his original attempted to do. This decision was surely a wise one. André trapped by accidents not of his making would be a mere pathetic creature. In so far as he approaches tragic stature, he does so because his fate is the result of his single fall from virtue, and because he understands and accepts this flaw.

Bland's failure to accept his friend's fate and M'Donald's failure to see it as tragic are the two poles of error in the play. Bland already appears as the emotional hero in the first scene, in which he passes from expressing fervent patriotism to expressing deep love for André. M'Donald marks his own character in the next scene: "I hope my every act/Has been the offspring of deliberate judgment" (*Act I, Scene 2*). Even his patriotism is rational—a position Dunlap had already endorsed: "I love this country for the sake of man." In "all the wond'rous deeds" of the Revolution he sees only "plain effects from causes full as plain." Also an echo of Dunlap's interest in Godwin is M'Donald's rejection of Bland's personal gratitude as unreasonable and selfish. Bland's reply to this recognizes M'Donald's role as the man of reason:

> Cold-blooded reasoners, such as thee, would blast
> All warm affection; asunder sever
> Every social tie of humanized man.
> Curst be thy sophisms! cunningly contriv'd
> The callous coldness of thy heart to cover,
> And screen thee from the brave man's detestation.
> (*Act IV, Scene 1*)

When Bland apologizes to M'Donald, he admits that he was "misled by passion" (*Act V, Scene 1*). In many ways, though, he has simply been seized by a new emotion, remorse; and M'Donald tells him "Remorse is vice," urging him to forget past vices and cultivate a present sense of virtue. In Bland's reliance on his heart rather than his head, he falls in with a long line of sentimental heroes. The saving grace of *André* is that Bland's values are questioned by the presence of M'Donald.

M'Donald's views are much like those of Dunlap at the time, but Bland's views carry equal force in the context of the play, and his sentimentality is like that of other Dunlap heroes. The true reconciler of the extremes is the General, for he sees man as a double creature: "His tide of passion struggling still with Reason's/Fair and favorable gale" (*Act I, Scene 2*). His inclination toward mercy is shown in every scene in which he appears. The scenes in which he refuses the pleas of Mrs. Bland that André be spared and of others that he be shot rather than hanged are omitted. The scene with Honora is included, and here the General's "heart is torn in twain" (*Act V, Scene 2*). His refusal to spare André is forced upon him by his duty to his country and his view of the long-range consequences of such an act; the report of the hanged American scout is introduced to justify this view. The General has been praised as one of the more successful stage portraits of Washington.[9]

But *André* is not a mere patriotic pageant, and Washington does not come on stage simply to make the audience applaud his entrance. Dunlap makes his idealized Washington the ideal figure of the play:

> By nature, or by early habit, grac'd
> With that blest quality which gives due force
> To every faculty, and keeps the mind
> In healthful equipoise.
>
> (*Act I, Scene 2*)

André is not a perfect play. Its weakness as a piece of theater is Dunlap's usual failure to provide much action to accompany his displays of sentiment. The issue of André's life or death is rarely in doubt. Even so, the weakest portions of the play are those invented to add theatrical effect. Bland does not fall in this category, for he merely personifies a response and attitude toward André. But his father's peril and his mother's and the young children's standing about being pathetic—these are not on a level with the rest of the drama in conception or execution. Dunlap's treatment of Honora's sudden arrival and final madness also seems perfunctory; these scenes have been written so many times before that Dunlap does not bother to rethink them. His blank verse descends to bathos in these scenes, while elsewhere it has a certain restrained force. The only Dunlap play to deal seriously with a serious subject, *André* may suggest the way in which the playwright Dunlap might have developed had not the manager Dunlap had more urgent necessities.

Some years later, Dunlap ravaged this artistic success and box-office failure to make an execrable but profitable patriotic play, *The Glory of Columbia—Her Yeomanry*. The case epitomizes Dunlap's theatrical career, as well as much of American theatrical history. Dunlap knew that his revision was only "a holiday drama . . . occasionally murdered for the amusement of holiday fools" (*Theatre*, II, 21). As a revision of *André*, it is criminal; as a separate treatment of the same theme, it is much inferior. It is best thought of as a comic opera on the theme suggested by its title— the virtues of sturdy American farmers. The scenes retained from André (nine out of the play's fifteen) are the weakest parts. Their serious tone, out of key with the rest of the play, give it the aspect of a comedy with tragic relief. Perhaps Dunlap kept them in order to lengthen the spectacle. Further cuts were made in performance.[10]

Early in the first act it seems possible that Dunlap is about to give a new serious version of the André case. It opens with Arnold's revealing to the audience that he needs cash and will sacrifice his principles to get it. Honest yeoman David Williams asks to be sent back to the fighting troops. He was glad to serve an invalid Arnold as an orderly, for Arnold had been a brave general; but Arnold is well now and somehow changed. When André comes, he is shocked to hear that he is within the posts of the American army, that he cannot return that night, and that he must return disguised. This situation follows the line of argument used by André's friends at the time—that André was ignorant of his position and acted only under Arnold's orders.

But in between these scenes is one which indicates the true direction of the new part of the play. David's sister Sally has come to visit him in camp, but he meets her on the way and tells her that even a camp of brave American soldiers is no place for his sister. In the last scene of the first act, David is taking her home when they are attacked by three unsavory English soldiers. Together—Sally is a spirited American lass—they beat them off.

John Paulding and Isaac Van Wert happen along, and the three
yeomen soldiers and Sally sing a song. By this point, it is obvious
that there is only one road in this play, so André's second-act capture by the three yeomen is no surprise. André offers them gold,
his pass from Arnold, high position in the British army; but nothing can swerve them from their duty, and André admires them for
it. The next scene combines the indifferent blank verse of the
General's soliloquy from *André* with a new prose passage in
which word reaches headquarters of the capture of André. We
next find Sally disguised as a soldier, singing and planning to
sneak into camp. She naturally runs into the three heroes on their
way back to camp from seeing Washington. David recognizes her,
and they pretend to think she is a spy and talk of hanging her on
the spot; this scene seems almost a parody of the capture of André. The joke finally over, they go to camp to join in a patriotic
chorus.

The third act of *The Glory of Columbia* is made up of snippets
from the first three acts of *André*, mainly those scenes including
Bland. His doffing the cockade has been cut, and the lines explaining his affection for André were omitted in performance. André's
admission that he lusts for glory is also cut, in line with the version
given in the first act. The fourth act of the revision includes three
scenes from the last two acts of *André*—two including Bland,
Honora, and André; one between the General and Honora. A
good deal of the sense and most of the seriousness of the original
is lost in this collection of fragments, but Dunlap tries to preserve
as many emotional outbursts as possible. The last act of the revision ignores the Bland-André plot entirely.

If *The Glory of Columbia* is regarded as a revised *André*, the
last act is anticlimactic; if it is a play about three brave common
soldiers, the third act is a disaster. The yeomen return in Act IV,
Scene 1, in which they capture a comic Irishman serving as a British soldier. Here the parody of the André capture may be intentional, for O'Bogg says he has observed how well the British have
treated Arnold and thinks he will desert himself, incidentally fleeing two wives and bad debts in New York. In the last act, O'Bogg
and the yeomen are present at the siege of Yorktown as Washington plans the final attack. O'Bogg is unhappy at the prospect—his
two wives have somehow arrived in Yorktown. Other soldiers
urge that revenge be taken for the cities the British soldiers have

sacked, but our sturdy yeomen tell their comrades to be resolute but merciful. In a spectacular scene, our heroes are shown taking the city. Washington makes a speech, and the curtain comes down on a song.

The Glory of Columbia has a rather unusual plot structure. Many works exhibit lines of action which are initially entirely separate but combined by the plot's end. Other works have parallel lines of action linked by relationships between characters—such as a comic romance between the servants of the hero and heroine. *The Glory of Columbia* has two principal lines of action, André's story and that of the yeomen. The two lines converge near the beginning of Act II and thereafter diverge, never to meet again. From the capture on, there are neither personal relationships nor shared themes to link the two stories. The only possible justification for the revised play is that the audience thus sees the equivalent of two bad plays instead of one. Quinn tells us that *The Glory of Columbia* is as a spectacle "above the average" (p. 88). This is a defensible judgment, but it only demonstrates the low quality of American patriotic drama in Dunlap's time.

No doubt the two bad plays which make up *The Glory of Columbia* would seem less horrible if they did not represent the bleeding remains of a relatively good play. Together with *Leicester, André* represents Dunlap's promise as a dramatist. If we are to trust his prefaces, both were begun when he was a young man, still in love with the theater and not yet charged with its burdens and overaware of its demands. Perhaps he could do no better; if so, he deserves credit for what he did accomplish. The American theater has since taken seriously many plays far less worthy than *André*. The need to produce rapidly plays suited to a provincial group of actors and to a public which preferred Kotzebue to Shakespeare, all while mixing in green-room quarrels and plunging into bankruptcy—this need could not have made it easier for Dunlap to advance beyond *Leicester* and *André*, if he were capable of doing so. Instead, he channeled much of his energies into making adaptations and translations.

CHAPTER *5*

Adaptations and Translations

WHEN dealing with the works of other authors, Dunlap believes "The practice of borrowing an original work from another nation, and accommodating it to our own, is a species of plagiarism"; and he warns that "The American dramatist, who steals the whole or part of an English play, cannot escape detection" (*Theatre*, I, 382). Dunlap is usually (but not always) conscientious about indicating the source from which he borrows, but he is often vague about the exact extent of the debt. We must make allowances for this vagueness in reading his claims that his plays are essentially original. But, although they are sometimes less original than he thought, Dunlap's free adaptations include some of his best efforts. His hard-earned knowledge of the theater enables him to extract the best from another's imaginings.

I Fontainville Abbey

Fontainville Abbey (1795), based on incidents found in Mrs. Radcliffe's Gothic novel, *Romance of the Forest,* helped introduce the characteristic Gothic atmosphere to American audiences. Dunlap's prefatory note acknowledges the debt to Mrs. Radcliffe and asserts that his play was written in 1794 and produced the next year. "Mr. Boaden's play of Fontainville Forest must have been performed about the same time in London." [1] The fact is that Boaden's play was printed in London in 1794 and that common deviations from the book make it certain Dunlap knew of Boaden's piece. Since there are only a few verbal parallels, it may be that he relied on written accounts or the word of actors or friends recently arrived from England. Even so, the prefatory remarks are misleading; Dunlap might well have been satisfied with the originality he does show and with the superiority of his version to Boaden's. [2]

As the play opens, LaMotte and his wife have taken refuge from a stormy night in an abandoned abbey. They are in flight from Paris and the creditors LaMotte has acquired at the gaming table. Madame is uncomplaining, but her husband's remorse knows no bounds. With them are their faithful servant, Peter, and a girl, Adeline, who is ill or exhausted. Seeking directions in the storm, LaMotte has come upon "a solitary house upon the heath" where a man of "fiend-like form" locks him in a room. The man drags the girl Adeline downstairs and demands at pistol point that LaMotte take her away. But the carriage wheel has broken, and they must stop for the night.

The method of this first act is to introduce a mystery (La-Motte's remorse), explain it at least partially, and then introduce another mystery (Adeline). The second act follows the same pattern. Adeline tells Madame that her unloving father was angry because she had resisted taking vows in a nunnery and would have shot her if LaMotte had not happened along. Peter reports they will be safe in the abbey, for the villagers think it haunted. It belongs to the Marquis de Montant, who rarely visits it. Someone is supposed to have been murdered in the east tower about the time he came into the estate. But the Marquis arrives to seek shelter from yet another storm. Impressed by Madame's account of their trials, he offers them his protection; but when LaMotte enters, the Marquis draws his sword. In a private conference off stage, he and LaMotte reach some bargain, which LaMotte will not reveal to his wife. Boaden puts their conference on stage, but Dunlap gains some suspense by not doing so. The Marquis is gallant with Adeline, who distrusts him. In a final soliloquy, LaMotte makes it clear that the Marquis has designs on Adeline, although we are not told why LaMotte must help him.

The third act merely deepens the mystery for the characters, although a reasonably alert audience should be able to understand the situation. A dream leads Adeline to a dark chamber where she sees a corpse in a chest and finds a parchment scroll which she soon reads aloud. Dunlap borrows a Boaden invention, having off-stage comments made while she reads; but Dunlap, preferring to suggest the supernatural but not present it, changes Boaden's Phantom to Peter. The scroll tells of a man slain by his brother and separated from his infant daughter. Peter comes in to tell Adeline that the Marquis was the murderer and now plans to take her to his castle with LaMotte's aid. She goes to seek Madame's help, passing the Marquis and LaMotte in conference. After the Marquis goes to exchange pleasantries with her, he returns much agitated, having recognized the seal of her mother, his murdered brother's wife. When he offers to redeem LaMotte's gambling debts if LaMotte will kill Adeline, LaMotte is horror-struck but agrees. This scene also shows Dunlap's debt to Boaden; the book has the Marquis make this request much later and as a frustrated lover. Boaden has the Marquis recognize the image of Adeline's mother on a locket, a notion no more probable than, and lacking the artistic economy of, Dunlap's use of the scroll.

The audience is allowed an intermission to ponder Adeline's peril. But, at the appointed hour of midnight, LaMotte stands outside her door, hears her innocent voice within, and cannot kill her. Boaden omits this scene, although it is in the plot from the novel and would have been an effective one for the actor playing LaMotte. In the forest at dawn, the Marquis forces LaMotte to admit he has not carried through his part of the bargain. Defying the Marquis's threats, LaMotte goes back to the abbey and confesses all to his wife and Adeline. Before they came to the abbey, he had robbed the Marquis in the woods; now he will hang for his crime. Adeline gives him the scroll as a keepsake.

The last act is in court, where LaMotte is on trial for robbery and slander. The scroll is presented, but without names it is too vague a document. Fortunately DuBose, Adeline's "father," enters and tells how the Marquis asked him to kill the girl. Trapped, the Marquis confesses that she is his brother's daughter and rightful heir. With a lack of repentance unusual in Dunlap, but true to the character in the book, the Marquis delivers a remarkable valedictory:

> Curse society and all its arts,
> To feter man and cramp him in his pleasure!
> It was my will to be a bold-fac'd villain,
> But I've been forc'd to play the hypocrite,
> And mingle my concerns with half-way fiends,
> And here's the end on't. Now I quit the mask,
> And curse ye all, with body, heart, and soul.
>
> (Act V)

The Marquis then tries and fails to stab himself. The attempt comes from Boaden's play, where it succeeds; in the book, he poisons himself successfully later. LaMotte is pardoned; in the book, he is merely banished instead of hanged, so Dunlap may follow Boaden here too. Adeline, of course, will restore LaMotte to prosperity with her new wealth.

The three versions—the novel, Boaden's play, and Dunlap's— contain many of the same incidents. Mrs. Radcliffe's center of interest is Adeline. There are many changes of scene, but everywhere Adeline is cherished, despite her habit of breaking into bad poetry at odd moments. Madame suspects LaMotte of loving her. LaMotte's son Louis loves her hopelessly. A young officer in the Marquis' regiment wins her love and is almost executed for attempting to save her. Boaden retains Louis and makes him the romantic hero who saves his family and Adeline by bringing officers of the law into the forest just as the Marquis is about to carry away LaMotte and Adeline. Louis gets Adeline as his reward, rather an improvement on the novel, where he does a great deal for her and gets nothing but heartbreak as his reward.

Dunlap's omission of Louis, as well as Adeline's other lovers, and his concentration of scenes in and around the abbey, makes LaMotte the focal point of interest in the play. LaMotte is a familiar figure in Dunlap, the man obsessed by his guilt. Adeline becomes an "orphan of the storm"; rejected by one father, she finds a new father and mother in the LaMottes, whom she addresses as if they were parents. She discovers the remains of her real father, and she is almost murdered by her adopted "father." Dunlap again selects elements from the common stock which deal with guilt over the murdered father and the desire to find a new father-protector. The enlarged role of LaMotte was probably designed for Hodgkinson, who produced the play. Mrs. Hodgkinson played Adeline, still the best female role; and the Hallams did not appear in the cast, though Hallam might have made a better Marquis than King, who "could do nothing but as instructed by Hodgkinson" (*Theatre*, I, 192). This again shows Hodgkinson as Dunlap's main link with the company.

Although Dunlap omits the phantom, the total effect of his changes is to emphasize the Gothic elements in the story. Mrs. Radcliffe's Adeline is exposed to horrors, but the worst are caused by the sex-mad Marquis; and much of the novel is given over to sentimental effusions about Nature, Love, and other abstractions. Like Dunlap, Boaden sets his action in the dark abbey and the thick forest; but his retention of a conventional love story dilutes the effect. By cutting the love interest, Dunlap focuses attention on guilt, terror, and mystery. It is always storming in Dunlap's play, without and within. His characters are never allowed to relax for more than a moment as they are hurried from crisis to crisis. It could easily serve as the script for a modern grade-B horror movie, although Hollywood would probably restore the love interest. The play has higher pretensions, and LaMotte's character is as well done as Henry Cecil's or Ribbemont's, but the work does not rise far above its source. Its good qualities are afterthoughts; its essential appeal to the audience is on the level of a thriller.

II   The Archers

Benjamin Carr wrote the music for *The Archers; or, Mountaineers of Switzerland* (1796), which gives Dunlap's opera a minor place in the history of American music. The play itself is derivative. In a preface, Dunlap acknowledges that he was given an English play to adapt and admits having retained from that play "three of the imaginary characters . . . the *Burgomeister, Lieutenant,* and *Rhodolpha:* I believe they are, however, strictly my own. The other similarities are the necessary consequences of being both founded on the same historical facts." [3] Any other borrowings are the result of a "treacherous memory" (p. vi). Dunlap's memory seemingly betrayed him; for, in taking characters from the other play, he also uses much of the plot in which they are involved.

Once again, Dunlap's adaptation shifts the focus of the play. His anonymous source, *Helvetic Liberty; or, The Lass of the Lakes,* has the Swiss patriots saved mainly by Marina, a Diana-like arrow-shooting heroine corresponding to Dunlap's Rhodolpha. Dunlap retains her, but he makes William Tell the central figure of his play. Hodgkinson took the part, and it may have been Hodgkinson who gave Dunlap the English play to adapt. Since both plays make use of the famous apple scene and have Tell kill the major villain, good sense alone may have dictated Dunlap's emphasis on Tell. He may have done some original research in the history of his subject—he appends "A Brief Historical Account of Switzerland" to the printed play—but the basic reason for the superiority of his adaptation to the original is that Tell is the logical hero.

Dunlap also introduces a comic subplot told in prose—the rest of the play is in blank verse. It features a merry basketwoman, Cecily (Mrs. Hodgkinson), and her lover, the bowl-merchant Conrad. The Lieutenant, a comic villain, forces Conrad and his donkey to join the emperor's army in the opening scene. After a farewell scene between Tell and his family, material from the original completes the first act. At the rebel camp, the leaders pledge to do or die. Rhodolpha tricks her father into granting her wish to go to war at the head of a troop of lady archers. The Marina of the source wins her point by argument; Dunlap may hope the use of feminine wiles will make his heroine seem less masculine. As in the original, one of the leaders, Arnold, loves her, a piece of plot evidently retained as an excuse for love songs.

The second act introduces the real villain of the play, Governor Gesler, who instructs the Lieutenant to arrest Tell. A quisling Burgomeister is baited by Rhodolpha and attempts to force her to bow to the governor's hat that is set on a pole, but she forces him to bow to her as the emblem of liberty. Conrad will not leave his guardpost to help the Burgomeister deal with Rhodolpha. Tell rouses the burghers to join the rebellion and refuses the Burgomeister's suggestion to collaborate with Austria. Cecily and Conrad escape, but the Lieutenant discovers Cecily and leads her away. "Why, you don't press women, do you?" she asks (*Act II, Scene 3*).

Tell's wife comes to plead for her husband's life, but Gesler is determined to have him hanged until a messenger arrives with word that Emperor Albert has been killed and Leopold has taken over. Gesler then substitutes the famous test. We are only told of this scene in *Helvetic Liberty;* Dunlap prepares for it by showing us Tell's family earlier; and, with his emphasis on Tell, he can show it on stage. In the next scene, which follows the original, the rebel leaders learn of the emperor's assassination and hope it will save Tell. This scene has no essential action and no new exposition of any significance; it is a kind of doubling resulting from Dunlap's insertion of the previous scene, which fills most of its func-

tions. The only remaining usefulness of this scene is that it reminds us its characters are still around—and permits them to sing
a song.

The third act has most of the action of the play. The first act is
mainly expository, and the second sets up the situations developed
in the third. Its first scene effectively combines two scenes separate in *Helvetic Liberty:* one in which Tell shoots the apple off his
son's head; one in which Gesler reneges on his promise of freedom
and rearrests Tell to take him across the lake to Leopold's army.
In the next scene, Tell arrives at the rebel camp after killing
Gesler and escaping. The final struggle now begins. In the town,
Conrad is captured and about to be shot through with arrows
when Rhodolpha and her female archers take the town and save
him. Even this scene represents a downgrading by Dunlap of the
heroine's role—in *Helvetic Liberty,* she saves her lover Arnold; in
The Archers, she saves only the comic Conrad, and Arnold comes
along to make sure the girls succeed in capturing the town. Everyone then goes to the main battleground, where Leopold's personal
bravery keeps the Austrians from defeat until he and Tell meet in
personal combat. They admire each other but know it is their duty
to destroy the animating spirit of the opposing army. Tell wins,
Conrad gets Cecily, Arnold gets Rhodolpha, Tell's family comes in
to embrace him, and everyone sings.

The Archers is too slight to claim much literary merit. The interest of the play depends on exciting action, for the characters
are neither explored nor developed. Tell is motivated by disinter-
ested patriotism from beginning to end; the Burgomeister is cor-
rupt and nothing more; Gesler is inexplicably cruel; and Arnold,
the chief singing role, has no character at all. Tell is too abstract a
figure for us to feel for him personally, although a father forced to
place his son in jeopardy is a sympathetic stage figure. We hate
Gesler because he is a simple stage villain, and we love the Swiss
because they are simple stage patriots.

Of little merit as literature, *The Archers* is an above average
piece of entertainment for its time, a 1796 equivalent of a modern
historical novel or of one of our less pretentious musical comedies.
The emphasis on Tell is not the only reason it is superior to its
source: the scenes are more rapidly paced and the dialogue is
considerably better. One of the most successful parts of the play is
the comic subplot, wholly Dunlap's invention. Although this sub-

plot is not well integrated into the action of the play—Conrad has two contacts with Rhodolpha and no important ones with Tell—it does serve a thematic function. Conrad represents the urban lower class, balancing the Swiss leaders, who are rural chiefs, and Tell, who is a city burgher. Although largely separate from it, the Conrad plot parallels the main plot. Like Tell, Conrad is a patriot; he is captured and sentenced to die; he survives to fight and win in the last great battle. The Lieutenant serves as Gesler's comic counterpart in the subplot. Cecily is a lower-class double for Rhodolpha, whose band of archers she joins.

Quinn has suggested (81) that the French Revolution inspired Dunlap's choice of subject, but it seems more likely that his interest was simply the result of being given a play to adapt. The French Revolution may have inspired the distinction between false and true liberty in the prologue, but the play makes the Swiss sound like American patriots. The Austrian governor (Gesler) is treated like a British royal governor, and the Burgomeister is like a Tory merchant on a governor's council. The patriots fight for their rights, their liberties, their country. Gesler and the emperor resemble the off-stage British in *André* who threaten the life of Bland's father and kill an American scout. Like André himself, Leopold is wholly admirable in his brief appearance, but he must die so that the Swiss may be free.

Dunlap reprints a letter from Thomas Holcroft concerning *The Archers*. It appears from the letter that the correspondence between Dunlap and Holcroft was most voluminous on Dunlap's part. Holcroft evidently refused earlier to read Dunlap's work in manuscript, having once been accused of plagiarism after reading an author's work; and he is unenthusiastic about the printed version of *The Archers:* "It proves you have made some progress; but it likewise proves, as far as I am a Judge, that much remains for you to accomplish. Common thoughts, common characters, and common sensations have little attraction: we must soar beyond them, or be contented to walk the earth and join the crowd" (*Theatre,* I, 310). Although he eventually accepted Holcroft's kindly but negative judgment, Dunlap at first believed that Holcroft might have found the play less common if "he had read the manuscript instead of the printed play" (*Theatre,* I, 311)—an opinion that seems to confirm that Dunlap was sometimes forced to revise his work to suit the actors. Nothing in *The Archers* as printed suggests today that it was ever more than a competent heroic drama with songs.

III   The Italian Father

The Italian Father (1799) was not announced as one of Dunlap's plays when first produced, a trick his predecessors had earlier played on the public when producing *Fontainville Abbey*. The public and even the actors were allowed to think it another of the manager's translations from Kotzebue, with the result that it was played well and applauded heartily. Dunlap himself calls it "the best of the many he has written" (*Theatre*, II, 106). His preface vaguely acknowledges that he has "enriched his work" from "old english dramatic literature." [4] His history makes the more specific admission that "Dekker furnished many of the finest passages" (*Theatre*, II, 106). Actually, the basic outline of the plot comes from Thomas Dekker's *The Honest Whore, Part II* (1630), and the few lines that Dunlap cites to show how he has imitated the style of Elizabethan drama are taken directly from Dekker.

In the opening scene of *The Italian Father*, Lodovico and his servant discuss his two former drinking companions, Hippolito and Beraldo. Several years ago Hippolito had married Beatrice despite the reluctance of her father the Duke, who at the same time forced Beraldo to marry Brazzo's daughter Astrabel, whom Beraldo had seduced. This summary is also one of *The Honest Whore, Part I*, but new names are given Dekker's Infelice (Beatrice), Matheo (Beraldo), Bellaforte (Astrabel), and Orland Friscobaldo (Brazzo). Lodovico and his servant come from the opening scene of Dekker's *Part II*. Later, Hippolito promises Astrabel that he will secure the Duke's pardon for Beraldo, who is about to die for his part in a tavern duel. Brazzo, still angry at his daughter, is letting Beraldo and Astrabel rot in poverty rather than help them; but, when Hippolito tests him by telling him that Astrabel is dead, the old man weeps. Told she lives, he regrets having wasted his tears on a harlot. This scene has been reworked from Dekker, who also contributes to the father's soliloquy in which he decides to go to his daughter in disguise. Dunlap's original contribution to the act is a pseudo-Elizabethan Fool, who performs some of the functions of Dekker's Lodovico and fills in time while the characters wait for the next relevant character to happen along the street.

Freed from prison, Beraldo, like his original in Dekker, is determined to "fly high" (*Act II, Scene 1*). The disguised Brazzo enters his son-in-law's service. He is touched by Astrabel's defense of her father; but, remembering that she was just as faithful before becoming a whore, he decides to have Hippolito test her character—the first major alteration by Dunlap of Dekker. Dekker's father enters Matheo's service to entrap him into an effort to rob himself; and Dekker's Hippolito, the virtuous hero of *Part I*, tries, because of simple lust, to seduce his friend's wife in *Part II*. At court, Lodovico's jests make Beatrice jealous of Astrabel; when Hippolito arrives, he can do nothing to allay her suspicions.

Act III, Scene 1, introduces a comic subplot that is original with Dunlap—at least in the sense that it is not found in Dekker. It was probably suggested by a trick played on Malvolio in *Twelfth Night*. The maid Leonora plots with the Fool to expose Lodovico, who will only see her at night and who, as a gentleman, would not think of marrying her. When Lodovico comes, she tells him her respectability can no longer afford meeting him openly. He must meet her at the chestnut grove, disguised in the Fool's coat. Hippolito brings a letter and some jewels to Astrabel, who conceals them from Beraldo. Beraldo is nevertheless suspicious enough to refuse a gift of gold and a new suit sent by Hippolito. Brazzo now suspects his daughter and has new respect for Beraldo, a plot twist which is Dunlap's improvement on Dekker. Astrabel, though, sends the letter and jewels back to Beatrice.

The last two acts are mainly Dunlap's. In the fourth act, Beatrice confronts Hippolito with the evidence and refuses to believe his explanations. Brazzo confirms them and is pleased to find his daughter true. No one has explained matters to Beraldo, who, thinking Lodovico a go-between for his wife and Hippolito, beats him, and then forces Hippolito into a duel. When Brazzo arrives to explain all, the main plot is over, but Dunlap drags the play out for another act with the aid of his subplot. In the chestnut grove, Lodovico is blinded and taught to imitate the Fool's voice. Brazzo, still disguised, has a long scene with his daughter in which he obtains her forgiveness for her father and promises to obtain his for her. The final scene finds Beraldo reinstated at court, Lodovico brought in blindfolded and made to embrace the Fool, and Brazzo reunited with his daughter. Lodovico gets pardon for his misbehavior; Leonora gets some money and the Fool for a husband.

The result of the changes Dunlap makes in Dekker's play is to substitute Dunlap's sentimental moralism for Dekker's sordid realism. The most important historian of American drama, Arthur Hobson Quinn, has even regarded Dunlap's play as superior "from the point of view of unity of construction, of swiftness of movement and stage effectiveness" (94). There are some gains. Dekker's father is so malevolent and his son-in-law so knavish that it is hard to become concerned about their reconciliation. Dekker's Hippolito is a curious combination of the noble fellow of *Part I* with the false friend and seducer required by the plot of *Part II;* no explanation is given for this inconsistency, and it is hard to see why his wife forgives him so readily. But Dunlap wins increased sympathy for his characters at the expense of their humanity. His Italian father is so soft at heart that we cannot understand how he has held himself so firmly in rein the past few years. His Beraldo's sense of honor mixes curiously with a knavishness left over from the original. If Dekker's Hippolito acts because of lust, Dunlap's is the participant in a purely stagy trick. Symptomatic of Dunlap's adaptation in general, this manipulation creates effective theater but makes the situation less lifelike.

The real weakness of Dunlap's version is precisely in "unity of construction." The comic subplot is attractive in its own right, but it has not even a thematic connection with the main plot. The last act is almost wholly anticlimactic. Defter craftsmanship would have assured that the main plot and subplot were resolved closer together, at least in the same act. There is no valid artistic reason for the delay in allowing Astrabel to share the knowledge gained at the end of Act IV by the other major characters. Brazzo's failure to reveal himself in Act V, Scene 2, is out of character. Dunlap sacrifices realism to extract a few more sentimental tears.

Viewed for a moment as an independent creation, *The Italian Father* shows Dunlap again seeking out the central situations of his first play, *The Father.* The mistaken jealousy of Beatrice recalls Mrs. Racket's dalliance with Ranter. More important, Dunlap again lavishes his greatest affection on his title character, a father separated from an only child. Conscious of her own guilt,

Beatrice wins reconciliation with the father; her husband also wins the older man's approval. This combines the search for a parent with the sense of guilt expressed in *Leicester* and *Ribbemont*. As usual in Dunlap, the end brings general forgiveness and absolution. The forgiveness comes easily, for the estrangements rest on misunderstanding. Beatrice should recognize that her husband is faithful by nature; Brazzo should recognize the essential goodness of Astrabel and Beraldo. The moral range of the play extends no lower than the folly exemplified by Lodovico, and the trick played on him lacks the cruelty of that played on Malvolio, since its victim's egotism is less malign. The raw force of Dekker is missing. To write a sentimental comedy in Elizabethan style, to take all the bawdry from a play called *The Honest Whore*—to do so is a tour de force; but the play Dunlap thought his best original drama is neither truly original nor his best.

IV   *Other Adaptations and Translations*

The other surviving adaptations by Dunlap are mainly inconsequential alterations of English plays to fit the New York stage.[5] Perhaps the most substantial change is the altered ending of John Till Allingham's *Mrs. Wiggins* (1803). The original ending has Old Wiggin say he can no longer endure his scolding wife. Dunlap contrives a sentimental ending; when their son announces that "When the one begins to scold, let the other be free to eat" (*Act II*), his parents are reconciled.

Of Dunlap's lost adaptations, the most significant would seem to be *Sterne's Maria; or, The Vintage* (1799)—evidently another of Dunlap's tributes to the sentimental side of Sterne. This play, based on an anecdote in Sterne's *Tristram Shandy* and with music by Victor Pellesier, "pleased and was pleasing," according to Dunlap, but it fell out of the repertoire after some original cast members left the company (*Theatre*, II, 93), and only a few songs and some extracts in Dunlap's history survive. Coad credits Dunlap with *Liberal Opinions* (1800), but Dunlap does not list it among his plays, so it may be only an adaptation for local use of Thomas Dibdin's *Liberal Opinions* (1800). Dunlap does list *The Flying Dutchman* (1827?) as his own, but this work is probably only an alteration of Edward Fitzball's play of that name.

As a translator, Dunlap is generally faithful without being lit-eral. He takes liberties in adapting foreign dramas to his stage, but he is not a creative translator. He is disposed to omit immorality but to allow foreigners to retain more than he would allow himself to display; his moralism shows itself most in a tendency to make the endings more didactic. Few of the plays he translated have great merit as literature, but they do cast light on Dunlap's methods as a translator and on the taste of the audience he faced.

Dunlap translated more plays of Kotzebue than of any other playwright. Probably the most popular of these translations was *The Stranger* (1798), a translation of Kotzebue's *Menschenhass und Reue*. Although no published copy of Dunlap's version survives, Myron Matlow has collected the available evidence and concluded that Dunlap "must have 'out-Kotzebue'd Kotzebue' in some of the sentimental scenes." [6] Matlow (43) also cites some apparent parallels between Dunlap's alterations and Sheridan's London version. Dunlap says he had seen only playbills of Sheridan's version; but, having observed other lapses of memory, we may wonder if he did not know more of it than he recalls. Dunlap also translated Kotzebue's absurd sequel, *Die edie Lüge*, as *The Stranger's Birthday* (1800). The first play tells of the misanthropic Stranger's reconciliation with his wife. In the sequel, the wife is tormented by the memory of her former infidelity; and her husband attempts to make her feel better by pretending he has got the servant girl pregnant. *The Stranger* was popular; its sequel, not.

Dunlap's version of *Das Kind der Liebe,* a tale of seduction righted by eventual marriage, was produced as *Lover's Vows* (1799). If this is the version published in New York in 1814 under his name as "Performed at the New-York Theatre," it is a reworking of an English translation, not an independent version, as his theater history claims. In the same year he produced a translation of Kotzebue's *Count Benyowski,* a father-lover-daughter triangle resolved in the father's favor, and one of Kotzebue's *Indians in England,* a father-son rivalry in love resolved in favor of the son. Previous British translations existed of both (Coad, 208); since Dunlap did not publish his version, we cannot tell if he used them. His last Kotzebue play of 1799 was *False Shame; or, The American in Germany.* It was not printed at the time but has since been made available in the American Lost Plays series in an edition edited by Coad (1940). An independent translation, it faithfully reproduces Kotzebue's tedious comedy. The "false shame" of the title prevents several of the characters from confiding in those who love them. As in some of Dunlap's own plays, the plot depends on the resulting misunderstandings.

Dunlap's adaptation of *Der Wildfang* as *The Wild Goose Chace* (1800) is also entirely his own; it is less exact in its rendering of the original, but the changes are mainly for the better. Love conquers all after yet another tangle of family relationships. Two other Kotzebue translations produced in 1800, *The Force of Calumny* (*Die Verläunder*) and *The Count of Burgundy,* were not printed. Dunlap may not have had a hand in the latter, for he never claimed it. British translations existed for both. *The Virgin of the Sun* (1800), about a pregnant vestal virgin in Peru, was taken from Kotzebue with the aid of a British translation. Coad argues (223) that the version actually produced was even closer to the British translation than the printed version published the same year.

The sequel to *The Virgin of the Sun* was the even more popular *Pizzaro in Peru; or, The Death of Rolla* (1800). The heroes are Peruvian patriots during the Spanish conquest, and splendid scenery was its great attraction. It became one of Dunlap's most popular efforts; during his tenure as manager, it was played more often than even *The Stranger* (Matlow, 269). Dunlap accurately states that it was "composed from the original and Sheridan's alterations" (*Theatre,* II, 123). *Fraternal Discord,* a Kotzebue translation which opened the fall season in 1800, was Dunlap's own choice as his best translation. It concerns two feuding brothers and their eventual reconciliation. The translation is independent and demonstrates his increasing ability to free himself of Germanicisms in his translations. His translation of *Blind Boy* (1800) has been lost to posterity, to no one's regret. It introduced to the American stage the young doctor who gets into difficulties and gets out of them by a brilliant operation (restoring the boy's sight).

In Dunlap's concentration on Kotzebue, he did not entirely ignore other German dramatists. One of his most successful translations was *Abaellino, the Great Bandit* (1801), from Johann Zschokke. The bandit is really a disguised young nobleman who ferrets out conspirators against Venice. Dunlap also produced unsuccessful translations of Schiller's *Don Carlos* (1799) and Joseph

Marius Babo's *Die Strelizen* (as *Peter the Great,* 1802), another
conspiracy play. An interlude about an old man who proves to be
The Good Neighbour (1803) was printed as "Altered from a
Scene of Iffland's."

Dunlap also translated a number of French melodramas and
farces, but he found no French author so popular with the audi-
ence nor so congenial in his sentimentality as Kotzebue. Several of
these have been printed. *Tell Truth and Shame the Devil* is a not
terribly original version of A. L. B. Robineau's farce, *Jérôme
Pointu,* about the exposure of a hypocritical lawyer. *The Voice of
Nature* (1803) is a sentimental melodrama taken directly from L.
C. Caignez's *Le Jugement de Salomon,* but influenced by John
Boaden's translation. *The Wife of Two Husbands* (1804) is from
Guilbert de Pixercourt's melodrama by way of British translations.
Thirty Years; or, The Gambler's Fate has been edited by Coad
(1940) in the same volume with *False Shame.* The protagonist's
final curtain speech summarizes the play: "See the miserable end
of a gamester!" The play is taken with little alteration from an
original by Prosper Goubaux and Victor Ducange. Other translations from the French are sentimental dramas of one sort or another.[7]

All of Dunlap's translations were produced after he became a
manager. Only a few were labors of love; the rest testify to his
need to provide popular attractions to keep his leaky enterprise
afloat. Most of these playwrights exploit a vein of sentimentality
difficult to take seriously today, although our own stage has its
Kotzebues. Dunlap lavished more skill, if not more invention, on
some of the adaptations; but these are no more great plays than
his translations. Dunlap introduced to the American stage the
plays of Kotzebue, the French melodrama, and the Gothic scene;
but these achievements belong to the history of our theater rather
than to that of our literature.

CHAPTER *6*

The Man of Letters

WHEN Dunlap was forced to look for a new source of income after his bankruptcy, he considered periodical work. Charles Brockden Brown, who knew what the prospects were, wrote him hoping to hear of plans "other than the literary one your letter mentions." Brown promised to contact a Philadelphia publisher: "But before that time, however, I hope you will get into some occupation more lucrative and permanent than anything of this kind can be."[1] Dunlap, who took Brown's advice, became a painter, although he was not to find it a particularly secure or lucrative profession. Over the period of years, however, he did a fair amount of writing. None of his prose works is written with a literary skill equal to that shown in his best plays; but some of them are readable still; several have some historical importance. We have already discussed the two most important of Dunlap's prose works, the histories of American art and American theater; but they are only part of a total body of work composed at odd intervals during a long life.

I   The Life of Charles Brockden Brown

Dunlap's biography of his friend Brown, published in 1815, is probably the most important of his minor prose works, although it is certainly not the most readable. Until more recent biographies by Harry Warfel (1949) and David Lee Clark (1952), Dunlap's biography remained "the best account of Brown that we have."[2] It is nevertheless a very unsatisfactory book. "It can hardly be called a biography," writes one critic; and another complains that "a feebler production than Dunlap's *Life* has seldom passed under the name of biography."[3] For many of its shortcomings Dunlap was not to blame. The biography was begun by Paul Allen, whose plan was to fill the bulk of two volumes with letters and selections from Brown's unfinished works. When Allen turned the work over to Dunlap, he renounced "all right to interfere";[4] but subscribers had been secured for the work as planned, and "the selections for the first volume had been made and printed" (I, iii). The selections are still useful to scholars of Brown, but they turn the biography into an odd, misshapen work. But, though the work is nearly unreadable and not always accurate, Dunlap's personal knowledge and his access to Brown's letters make his volumes "the basis for all subsequent studies of Brown."[5]

The first volume of the biography portrays the life of Brown through 1797; it is the story of a man searching for a vocation and finding it in writing. The second volume, which covers his life from 1798 to his death in 1810, tells of his successful years; but it begins with the death of his friend Smith, which anticipates Brown's own early death. The natural unity of the biographical portions is, however, lost in the writing. The biographical portions are overshadowed by the selections, which form the bulk of both volumes. Even in the biography proper, Dunlap quotes at length from Brown's letters and journals and gives unnecessarily lengthy extracts from papers given before a literary club and from political pamphlets. The biography becomes mere commentary, even in the second volume, which is partitioned into separate sections of biography, of letters not used in the biography, and of selections from Brown's manuscripts.

Dunlap is forced to acknowledge at the outset that Brown has "not attracted that universal notice, nor excited that interest, even among his countrymen generally, which would authorize the writing of his life upon the principle of gratifying public curiosity" (I, 9). His justification for writing is to call attention to Brown as one of the first Americans to enter "the world of fiction and the painful path of public amusement or instruction" (I, 9). He also pays tribute at the beginning and throughout to Brown's personal merits and artistic talents. As in Dunlap's histories of the arts, he tries to transcend the merely commemorative by placing his subject in a historical setting, but fails to sustain the effort.

Dunlap also admits that Brown's life was not filled with exciting actions. Such actions, he argues, even if present in his subject's life, might well distract the reader from more important influences on his life as a writer. "The *incidents* of an author, are his ideas,"

Dunlap writes (I, 68)—echoing Brown's own views on biography.[6] Dunlap cites with approval a friend's remark that "in the life of a literary man, character is biography" (I, 67). But Dunlap's intentions are once again more admirable than his execution. He does, as he promises, omit the dull details of financial negotiations with publishers, and the many letters he prints add to our knowledge of Brown's character. But he devotes only a few pages to Brown's youth. He tells us Brown was often moody and radical in his opinions, but he cites few specific examples of either quality. Of the courtship and marriage, which seem to have changed Brown greatly, Dunlap has little to say. Of some of these matters Dunlap may have been ignorant; about others, he may be exercising the reticence of a friend. Whatever his reasons, he leaves the reader with a view of Brown that is less clear than that of many of the minor artists given capsule biographies in his art history.

Dunlap's comments on Brown's works display the same criteria of judgment found in his major histories. His feeling for craftsmanship is disturbed by Brown's occasional failure to keep track of elements in his fiction. In *Arthur Mervyn*, for example, Dunlap objects to "an episodical incident, altogether useless, and such a blot upon the story as could only have arisen from the author's writing, without revision, and forgetting in some measure that part of his work already consigned to the printer" (I, 68). He complains that Brown deliberately left loose plot ends, so that he might "pursue his subject still further, as his future leisure or inclination might dictate," leaving all the novels more or less "unfinished" (I, 259).

The moralism so prominent in Dunlap's histories plays a less important part in his discussion of Brown's novels. It is probably most apparent in his attempt to explain away the apparent immorality of some of the views expressed in *Alcuin*, especially in the part originally suppressed but reprinted in the biography. He quotes a friend who maintains that Brown's doubts concerning marriage are advanced only to demonstrate the sophistry of the arguments used—an analysis clearly in conflict with a passage reprinted from Brown's journal in which he boasts that the dialogues discuss the topic of marriage "with some degree of subtlety at least" (I, 107). Dunlap himself seems to regard the dialogues as an expression of a youthful skepticism as yet unrestrained by common sense. He is able to praise *Edgar Huntly* as "full of moral instruction" (II, 38) and to note that the characters in *Clara Howard* are "eminently moral and delicate" (II, 42).

Dunlap's realism makes it difficult for him to accept Brown's heroes' "incredible and mysterious adventures" (I, 261). In *Ormond,* he finds Ormond's villainy too sudden to be convincing. Concern for probability may also be behind Dunlap's complaint that *Edgar Huntly*—which he consistently spells *Huntley*—crowds its events "into an unnecessarily short period." About *Wieland,* he raises some mild objections to the use of spontaneous combustion and ventriloquism to provide natural explanations for seemingly supernatural occurrences. But such specific complaints are all too rare; Dunlap evidently feels he must devote much of his time to providing plot summaries for readers unfamiliar with Brown's works.

In his evaluations, Dunlap displays the same ability to rise above personal friendship which was to annoy some first readers of his histories. His taste in praising *Wieland* above Brown's other novels and in dismissing *Jane Talbot* with a sentence is unexceptionable. He may be too kind to *Clara Howard,* but on the whole he may even underrate Brown's work: "His novels are evidences of what he *might* have done, not of what he accomplished" (I, 161). We might say the same of Dunlap's biography, for considering Dunlap's friendship with Brown, we learn too little of the man. Still, writing volumes conceived by another and designed to memorialize one of his dearest friends, Dunlap might have done worse. As a firsthand account of one of our first professional men, his biography is indispensable, despite its faults.

II   The Life of George Fred. Cooke

Dunlap's biography of Cooke is superior to his biography of Brown in almost every particular. This superiority is not, however, to be attributed to any growth of ability in Dunlap as a biographer; the first edition of the Cooke biography was published in 1813, two years before the Brown. Contemporaries of the great English actor recognized the book as well done. The Philadelphia manager Wood called it "a faithful portrait" by "a close observer and a truthful writer." [7] Lamb was said to have praised it highly, and Byron delighted in its liquor-soaked pages, marvelling "that a man should live so long drunk, and next, that he should have found a sober biographer." [8] A modern student of American biographies calls it "a remarkably good biography for its time." [9] For writing it, Dunlap finally found a publisher willing to pay him three hundred dollars for the American rights. Despite its superior merit, it seems less important today than the Brown biography; Brown, less interesting as a man, is of more interest to us as an artist.

Cooke may actually have been a greater artist than Brown; indeed, Dunlap speaks of his genius with fewer reservations than he shows in discussing his friend. But Cooke lived long before the camera could record a performance; his art is lost to us. Through his drunkenness, he threw away, moreover, any chance to make his mark on theatrical history as an actor-manager. Cooke undoubtedly recognized this failure; and, when he "rather sportively" (I, iii) asked Dunlap to be his biographer, he may have hoped Dunlap could equal the lives of Garrick and Macklin mentioned as honorable predecessors in Dunlap's preface. He may have hoped also that Dunlap would set forth his claim to stand in the line of those great English actors. That Cooke had some thought for posterity is indicated by his having started a chronicle of his theatrical career and by his having carried it forward to 1807.

The first volume of Dunlap's biography covers the period of this chronicle, supplementing it with journals Cooke had kept at the time. It begins with Cooke's birth in 1756 and chronicles his long years in the provinces, his London triumph in 1800–1801, and his failure to keep when drunk the public favor won while sober. The volume ends with Cooke in prison for debt, having squandered a good season's wages. The first third of the next volume takes Cooke out of jail to his meeting with Thomas Cooper in 1810; for this, Dunlap relies on journals. For the negotiations leading to Cooke's American tour and for the tour itself, Dunlap is able to draw on more personal sources. The last two years of Cooke's life thus occupy nearly a third of Dunlap's pages. Dunlap justifies this by saying "The closing scenes of such a man's life are like the catastrophe of a drama, more interesting and impressive than the preceding acts"; then he more practically adds: "These scenes have come immediately under my observation, and the description of them is more peculiarly the gift which I could alone make to the public" (I, viii).

The biographical purpose implied by Dunlap's preface is mimetic and thus consistent with his general notions about art and literature. He hopes "to exhibit a faithful picture of this extraordinary man" by "portraying the image formed in my mind by the knowledge I possess of Mr. Cooke" (I, v). The recognition that his image of Cooke rather than Cooke himself is the object of imitation is a theoretical nicety uncommon in Dunlap. Dunlap's moralism sees in Cooke's life "an impressive lesson to every reader" (I, v). Its interest is considered as lying not in Cooke's having been an actor but in his having been "placed in situations interesting to his fellow men" (I, vi). The ephemeral nature of the actor's work makes it impossible to turn from a biography to the work of art as we can with other artists. This factor encourages the biographer to seek interest for his biography in details of personality and permanent significance in its fidelity to life and comment on it. So Dunlap presents Cooke as an example of those whose "talent and genius" is insufficient, "without the aid of prudence, to procure happiness for their possessor, or to benefit mankind; otherwise than by the lesson which their deplorable failure imparts for the instruction of others" (II, 409-10).

To create his portrait, Dunlap relies heavily on Cooke's papers, which are fortunately much more colorful than the letters and journals quoted in his Brown biography. As many as twenty or thirty pages at a time are devoted to direct transcriptions of Cooke's journals. Dunlap does not, however, simply transcribe all that he found. Even when quoting at length, he cuts what seems to him irrelevant. "Even yet too much may be retained," he writes; "but there is a kind of near and intimate view obtained of a man, through the medium of a particular journal of even his uninteresting actions, which ought not to be altogether withheld from the public" (II, 36). He also pauses from time to time to explain or comment on passages he transcribes. Although some details can be of interest only to scholars concerned with the history of the English theater, Dunlap's use of Cooke's journals is generally successful. Something of Cooke's robust charm found its way into his journals, in comments like this on the rascality of theater managers: "From the first theater to the barn (with the exception of only two, within my knowledge) their intentions are the same, altho' happily, there are many blockheads among them, who cannot execute those intentions" (I, 381).

The last third of the book relies heavily on Dunlap's diaries, but Dunlap remains a reasonably unobtrusive biographer, despite his moralizing. He admits he hoped to "have a powerful influence" over Cooke's conduct, but he concedes the hope was probably mere "self-flattery" (II, 244). He pictures his effort to keep Cooke sober as having been seldom successful, and he records only a few of the occasions on which Cooke expressed his gratitude: "I owe my life to you. They see you with me & they think I can't be bad. they spare me for your sake. Who's that with him? Dunlap. Ah its all well" (*Diary*, II, 444). Nor does the biography reflect the frustration and exasperation Dunlap sometimes felt while trying to keep Cooke from his vices. "The old wretch went out to his Whores again as soon as I was gone," Dunlap wrote in his diary (II, 443); but the trip and the tone ("old wretch") find no place in the biography.

In fact, whether from concern for Cooke's reputation or for the sensibilities of the reader, Dunlap regularly omits references to Cooke's sins of the flesh. Where the diary (II, 444) has "while I was absent C thought I had gone to bed & ordered a Coach to go to the brothel," the biography (II, 326) has Cooke ordering his servant "to go for a coach" with no destination stated or implied. Elsewhere in the biography, Dunlap explicitly defends Cooke against some charges. He denies that Cooke ever asked for return of money given to a charity. Cooke only wished to be sure the person given a draft "was an authorized agent" for the charity (II, 290). Cooke's oft-repeated claim to have fought for the British during the American Revolution is attributed to congenital playacting rather than to madness or lying (II, 375–77).

The effect of Dunlap's reticence about whorehouses and bad debts is to make drunkenness Cooke's master weakness and the key to his failure to make more of his great talents. The book takes its form from the conflict between Cooke's great abilities and the irresponsible behavior he was led to by drunkenness and bad companions. Dunlap argues that he deals with Cooke's intemperance, not for its own sake, but because of the interest of the ingenuity Cooke showed in extricating himself from the difficulties he brought on himself and because of the moral lesson to be derived from his ultimate inability to do so (II, 206–7). He also says that a discussion of Cooke's drunkenness may be "expected from me" because his subject's vice was so widely known (II, 352). He ties the conflict between Cooke's talents and vices to a patriotic theme by asserting that Cooke's visit to America "probably lengthened his life more than any circumstance likely to have happened in his native country" (II, 168) by taking him away from old haunts and challenging him to live up to his great reputation as an actor.

Dunlap's comments on Cooke's acting also assume a mimetic theory of the histrionic art. The actor should control "every minute movement of body and inflection of voice" so as to give a "just representation" of the character (II, 404). The untutored Cooke's method was evidently less "technical." "As if by intuition" he was capable of "seizing the perfect image of the person he would represent, and identifying it with his own feelings, so as to express every emotion designed by the author, as if that emotion was his own" (I, 240–41). Cooke is praised for owning to the influence of "the happy efforts of other artists in their representations of nature—but he never lost sight of nature in his own exhibitions of character" (II, 192). Cooke was an actor of great emotional power, and Dunlap liked him best in strong, tragic parts which gave Cooke scope for "His exhibitions of the strongest and most malignant passions of human nature" (I, 206). Nevertheless, Dunlap's preference for realism appears in his praise of "the natural and unaffected tone" of Cooke's handling of verse on stage (I, 159).

Dunlap knows there is artifice behind an actor's naturalness. He rejects the "absurdity" of assuming the actor must possess the qualities of the character he portrays (II, 194). His ideal actor achieves a just representation by assuming those qualities. As a practical matter, he acknowledges that an actor's face and figure are not under his control; he ranks Cooke as Kemble's superior in parts where nobility of form and countenance are of little importance but as his inferior where those are demanded (I, 156–57, 175). Dunlap does not record many details of Cooke's performance. He regrets this lack, "but perhaps the reader may have cause for congratulation that he spared such minute criticism" (II, 179). Where Dunlap does record such details, he shows a liking for effective theatrical gestures of a rather stylized sort, but the terms in which his praise is couched continue to suggest modern "method" acting: "All depends upon the perfect unison of the mind and body, and the mind and body being identified with the character" (II, 401).

Dunlap's life of Cooke does not tell us all he knew about the man, but both the biographer and the journals he reprints are more revealing than in the Brown biography. Moreover, the relatively lesser intrinsic importance of Cooke means that our thirst for information is less and our concern for the purely literary qualities of the biography itself is greater. We are left free to enjoy such well-constructed scenes as that in which Cooke's eloquence first charms and then puts to sleep William Godwin, to whom Thomas Cooper has introduced him. Even Dunlap's recurring homilies on the evils of drink have some justification since they unify an otherwise anecdotal narrative around a single theme. Regarded in this way, Dunlap's biography of Cooke, although lacking the historical importance of his biography of Brown and his major histories, is one of his most readable works.

III   Thirty Years Ago; or, The Memoirs of a Water-Drinker

Although Dunlap's first and only novel was published in 1836, he had earlier shown an interest in the form. An undated letter from William Godwin advises him that his chances of finding a London publisher for a projected novel are better than for dramas unperformed on the London stage.[10] This novel may have been the "Anti-Jacobin," mentioned earlier and also known as "The Innovator" or "Harry Colbert" after its rationalist hero. Dunlap's diaries of 1797–98 indicate he was also working on a similar but apparently different novel called "Charles Thompson." An 1833 letter to James Fenimore Cooper mentions another novel: after it had been "bandied about between Casey & Harpers, the latter agreed to give me 500 dollars for it, to publish it when they please (or to use their language 'stick in somewhere' . . .) and I suppose pay me when they please." [11] This novel may be the one eventually published as *Thirty Years Ago; or, The Memoirs of a Water-Drinker*, although Harper did not publish it, and Dunlap held the copyright in his own hands.

The novel displays the same deficiencies in over-all construction that plague Dunlap's plays. After some forty-five pages have gone by, he announces, "as we have promised to begin at the beginning, we hasten to commence our story" (I, 46). Even this belated promise is ill-kept, for most of the first volume of the novel is devoted to introducing and then to giving the past histories of characters both important and unimportant. The water-drinking hero, Zeb Spiffard, had a mother who drank to excess. The oldest and ugliest of her children, he is now a popular comedian with the New York theater under Thomas Cooper's management; and he has recently married a stately tragic actress older and taller than himself. Both his new wife and her mother are drunkards, but they at first succeed in hiding their vice from him. The novel's heroine, Emma Portland, is a bland young cousin of the new Mrs. Spiffard and is in love with a dull young clerk, Henry Johnson, whose principal occupation is caring for his sick mother. In the first volume, overheard remarks make Spiffard suspect his wife; a cloaked figure grabs at Emma as she visits backstage; and Spiffard faints at a party when he sees a woman who strongly resembles his mother. It is his mother's sister, a lady with a scandalous past who is now married to a fake general.

In the second volume, the main plot, such as it is, is reinforced by an extended hoax played upon the hero by his young friends. Worried about a "duel" they have arranged for him, Spiffard becomes sullen and irritable, convincing his wife that he knows of her drinking and driving her to drink more. Meanwhile, the mysterious villain accosts Emma in an alley; later, she is lured to a room in the slums by an appeal to her charitable instincts. Both times she is saved by the fortuitous appearance of her beloved Henry. In another subplot, Spiffard's aunt dies an alcoholic, revealing enough in her frenzy to tarnish the fake general's reputation. Called to the bedside by the author's whim, Emma recognizes the general's voice as that of her attacker; but she is too saintly to expose him. Spiffard discovers his wife drinking and leaves her, only to return to find she has committed suicide. He leaves the theater to become a minister and founder of temperance societies; the fake general leaves the country; and Emma and Henry, now a firm partner instead of mere clerk, are wed.

Yet another subplot, one which concerns George Frederick Cooke, is loosely tied to the novel by the temperance theme. Cooke displays the ill-effects of overdrinking in scenes drawn from memory and Dunlap's diaries. Cooke is allowed to die bravely; but his death, like that of Spiffard's aunt and wife, is used to illustrate the effects of debauched living on otherwise well-favored individuals. Early in the novel, Dunlap assures us that, in dealing with historical figures like Cooke and Cooper, he assigns no actions "at variance with the general character of the person" (I, 7). Perhaps it is within this limit to assign the thrice-married Cooke an extra wife, as Dunlap does; it is Henry's mother, who years ago fled from Cooke's drunken rages, and has never forgiven him. A willingness to disregard the laws of probability enables Dunlap to arrange a meeting in which Cooke is too sick and drunk to recognize her, and she is too unforgiving to reveal herself to him.

Even less closely related to the rest of the novel is a line of action of some interest because it returns to Dunlap's early concern with father-son relationships. Spiffard, who is often attracted to older men, makes friends with a merchant named Littlejohn, one of whose sons is dead. They visit the other son in an insane asylum, where the madman denies that there is any special virtue in filial love; like so much else in Dunlap, this incident may stem from the guilt felt at his estrangement from his father and the father's death. In the novel, it develops that Littlejohn is Henry's employer. Having seen his employee once or twice asleep at his desk, the "benevolent merchant" (II, 135) has withheld a half-year's wages from his salary. Finding out that Henry was moonlighting to support his mother, he releases the funds and makes amends by taking Henry into partnership. Henry, estranged from his real father (Cooke), is thus accepted by a surrogate father. The madman son also recovers at the end of the novel and resumes his normal vocation—that of a clergyman! This links him to the orphaned Spiffard. Considering the possible Oedipal roots of the father theme in Dunlap, it is interesting that Spiffard marries a woman bigger than himself, that he faints at the sight of his mother's look-alike sister, and that this formerly mad clergyman is improbably married to yet another Spiffard aunt at the end of the novel.

"It is, perhaps, unnecessary to say," Dunlap writes at the end, "that a moral is to be drawn from the story of Zebediah Spiffard" (II, 220). The reader is given little opportunity to escape the moral lesson of the book. Indeed, its rambling structure and improbable incidents can best be defended by seeing it as didactic in form—a novel in which the incidents are selected and arranged to prove a thesis rather than to satisfy purely esthetic criteria. This temperance novel is at times almost a temperance tract: "The murders (including suicides and deaths by dueling) that are the fruits of intemperance, constitute far the greater portion of those which stain the records of the judicial, or private history of society" (II, 207).

As usual, Dunlap's moralism is accompanied by a mimetic theory of art: his story is "copied from real life" (I, 69), and to omit all unhappiness from his story would "give a false picture of human life" (II, 69). Insistence on his story's realism makes Dunlap deny that he is using traditional artifices even while doing so. A hunting squire named Lovedog was "taught something at school about Moses and Christ, but had forgotten whether they were racers or pointers" (I, 55). Of his name Dunlap asserts, "This is not a coined name to express character . . . and that it should denote the bearer's character, is not our fault" (I, 52). Dunlap introduces stage low-comedy types and then claims, "If I have introduced an Irishman and a Yankee, it is because my scene is in New-York; and in New-York one cannot turn a corner but an Irishman is at one elbow and a Yankee at the other" (I, 33). Even when he admits to using novelistic conventions, Dunlap is self-conscious about them. The use of flashbacks "being the established mode, we shall in all humility follow it" (I, 198).

The moralism and mimeticism of the histories are again accompanied in the novel by a nostalgic tone, as indicated by the title *Thirty Years Ago*. The nostalgia is not really undermined by occasional reminders that those were the bad old days—"There were then no *temperance societies*. Gentlemen—yes, *gentlemen*, did not think themselves degraded by drunkenness" (I, 124). Despite the moral lessons drawn from their intemperance, the companions of Dunlap's younger days are treated well. Cooke is rather more sympathetically pictured than in the biography, and Thomas Cooper is excused from his part in the hoax on Spiffard.

The nostalgic tone is understandable, since the life of the protagonist has a number of parallels with Dunlap's own: he leaves home young; he learns the delights of a good library from an older man (an uncle); he is apprenticed to a dull profession (the law), but devotes his time to the theater instead. Additionally indulged in a visit to England, he cultivates his talents as a singer; although an honest man, he enters theatrical life; his financial prospects for the future are lost—though not through his own naïveté, like Dunlap's; he leaves the theater about the time Dunlap severed his own connection; even his comic appearance may derive from Dunlap's consciousness of his own partial blindness. Littlejohn also has some of Dunlap's traits and opinions; he may have himself in mind in defending Littlejohn as a companion for a younger man: "Age is garrulous; but this, if the memory is perfect and the love of truth strong, may be a source of great profit to youth" (I, 129).

Many incidents and characters come directly from Dunlap's past and can be found in his histories and diaries. The hoax on Spiffard comes from one Thomas Cooper and others played on the comedian William Twaits, who may also have served as a model for Spiffard in other respects. The visit to the insane asylum Dunlap made himself in the 1830's. Some of the inmates he saw then appear in the novel's visit, including the young man reading the poems of Philip Freneau. To this Dunlap adds a remark charged with personal significance: "Poor Philip! He is almost forgotten, like some other of our literary pioneers" (I, 144). Littlejohn's son Thomas, who died while brooding on death, may have been suggested by Brown. More recent friends are also given their due; the reader is twice referred to works by James Fenimore Cooper (I, 48; II, 208).

Although temperance is its controlling theme, the novel is almost a compendium of the views Dunlap held in his later years. His respect for religion is seen in an unfavorable treatment of Lovedog and his atheistic wife, and perhaps in the treatment of Littlejohn's mad son (the rationalist as madman). But in other passages Dunlap objects to the fanaticism of unlettered Fundamentalists and praises the tolerant tradition of Roger Williams; for Dunlap, "religion is benevolence" (II, 171). His patriotism finds frequent expression—Spiffard's father made his great error in marrying someone reared in England and exposed to its evils. Dunlap also favors the cause of the Indians and the practice of not executing criminals judged insane. He expresses once more his aversion to slavery. He takes mild exception to the politics of the "naturalized" (II, 217), and he pokes fun at a Revolutionary War colonel who lives for years off laurels he may or may not have earned. The framework of the novel is loose enough for most of Dunlap's prejudices to find admission.

Van Wyck Brooks says the novel is "lively and vivid in spots but hasty and disorderly, like all of Dunlap's works." [12] The usually sympathetic Coad says it was "well-received" at the time but "is Dunlap's least praiseworthy book" (179, 177), a judgment which seems to overlook some of the political histories to be dealt with in the next few pages. The novel has no special merit as art. It does have Dunlap's sense of life as "a tragi-comedy" (II, 199) in which the wicked sometimes prosper and the good sometimes die and in which a real George Frederick Cooke and an imaginary Mrs. Spiffard may possess both great talents and great weaknesses. Many of the novel's incidents are absurdly improbable, dragged in only to twist the plot or prove the thesis, but the world in which they occur is richer and more complex than in most of Dunlap's dramas. Both his monitory purpose and his use of personal recollections probably helped him mitigate the air of benevolent sentimentality still very much a part of the novel. Dunlap had a hard life, but he retained his enthusiasm for living—though in his last years he lived increasingly in the past. The reader willing to be patient with his novel's faulty construction and slow pace will not go wholly unrewarded.

IV The Political Histories

Compared with Dunlap's excursions into military and political history, even his biography of Brown seems interesting, and even his novel and the Cooke biography seem important. None of these histories is more than intermittently readable. Only one represents more than hackwork, the two-volume *History of the New Netherlands, Province of New York, and State of New York, to the Adoption of the Federal Constitution* (New York, 1839–40). Dunlap worked on this book for some time; a letter to James Fenimore Cooper in 1836 already finds Dunlap "rummaging old newspapers for (what you have called) my gossiping history of this City of New York" [13]—although the final version is a state history, the focus is still on the city. He did not live to complete it: the posthumous second volume, assembled from materials written before Dunlap died, notes that "the greater part of the first volume was printed after the author was attacked with a disease, which ultimately proved fatal" (II, 7). Proofreading devolved upon an editor, probably John Dunlap (Coad, 267), who was unfamiliar with the work and its subject, and thus unable to complete what Dunlap left unfinished.

Dunlap's intentions are once more admirable: to show "one continued chain of events" leading "to the great results which we now witness" (I, 312). But his desire to include "every fact that can be rescued from oblivion" keeps him from achieving any such historical synthesis. A letter to a friend in early 1839 asserts that "I will confine myself to two heroes, Petrus Stuyvesant for my first volume, and George Washington for my second." [14] The narrative would have benefited by the use of such focal figures, although there is a considerable time-gap between them. As it stands, Stuyvesant is given credit for "his superior wisdom and energy" (I, 85), but he does not even dominate the single chapter in which he stands. Washington, presented in more heroic terms, is obviously important in the military history of the Revolution, but the book remains a chronicle of events, not men.

Dunlap's antiquarian bias, excusable in the major histories because of Dunlap's unique sources of information, is fatal in this work. Here Dunlap is dealing with sources available to all, and his method was already outmoded in his own time. At times he appears to share historian George Bancroft's sense of a guiding Providence: "That power which had frustrated the designs of Arnold, and decreed the destruction of Sir Henry Clinton's agent, for purposes beyond our ken, interposed to preserve the arch-traitor, Arnold, from immediate punishment" (II, 189). Dunlap's Providence works for its own inscrutable ends; the historian is unable to read the pattern and give the reader a meaningful narrative.

As in the histories, Dunlap's antiquarian approach leads him to strive for accuracy. He uses the works of other historians, but he has obviously spent some time working with the materials available in the library of the New York State Historical Society. His use of his predecessors is not altogether uncritical; he is particularly scathing about a colonial historian who "praises his father's eloquence, when he persuaded the house of representatives to reject the votes of the Israelites, because their fathers, seventeen hundred years past, had demanded the death of one condemned by their rulers" (I, 318). On occasion, Dunlap may have sought special sources of information; for he cites a conversation with a confidential clerk in Clinton's office about the Arnold case. Not simply taking the ex-clerk's word for it, Dunlap finds support in a passage in Clinton's letters. At other times, his use of sources is uncritical. Nevertheless, he has influenced some later historians and was used by James Fenimore Cooper to provide historical background for *Satanstoe*.[15]

Although written by a sick and dying man, the history of New York is the most readable as well as the most scholarly of Dunlap's political histories. Readers interested in Dunlap may find it casts some light on his beliefs in his last years. Of special interest is the treatment of the Arnold-André affair. Dunlap now writes as if he had never shared in "the fictitious admiration of this young gentleman, which was created principally to cast odium upon General Washington and the sacred cause of an insulted people" (II, 188). André is "handsome and accomplished" (II, 191), and he dies well; but Dunlap stresses his involvement with Arnold's plans. He compares him unfavorably to Nathan Hale, who spied for patriotism rather than for glory or promotion, who risked his life willingly, and who was treated badly by his captors. Citations to the writings of Jared Sparks suggest that the historian's interpretation of the Arnold conspiracy helped change Dunlap's.

The political views expressed are those found in other Dunlap works: slavery is an unmitigated evil, and Dunlap once again invokes the name of slaveless Thomas Bartow "blessed be his memory" (I, 323n.); but, like Bancroft, Dunlap blames the British for fastening the curse of slavery on America. Its abolition is given as one of the reasons for the "prosperity and greatness" of New York (I, 320). Dunlap also is sympathetic to the Indians, whom he regards as often "Provoked by dishonest traders and maddened by rum" (I, 68).

Coad (68) asserts the history betrays a Federalist bias, but Dunlap's Federalism is that of the *Federalist Papers*, the days when Alexander Hamilton and James Madison collaborated, not of the most narrowly based political party that came into being in the 1790's. He condemns the Articles of Confederation and praises the Constitution, but he shows few of the common Federalist prejudices in domestic affairs. He sees the state's history as a long conflict between would-be aristocrats and true democrats, and Dunlap is on the side of "the people" (I, 298). He is also far more anti-British than in his histories of the arts.

Dunlap's two-volume *History of New York, for Schools* (New York, 1837) draws upon materials collected for the more impor-

tant work. Frankly imitating the format and proposing to carry
forward the history of an earlier primer on New York as a colony,
the book is written as the conversation of four incredibly bright
childen with their learned great-uncle Betterworth, and it carries
the state's history to the end of the Revolution. The uncle, like
Dunlap, is seventy-one; and like Dunlap, he is working in the li-
braries on New York history: "I daily add some fact, or overthrow
some error" (1855 ed., I, 1). The link with Dunlap adds a certain
poignancy to the uncle's belief that "as I am out of date—a thing
of past tense—I am only fitted to prepare the children for the
future" (I, 1).

The contents of Dunlap's textbook parallel those of his later
history of the state and are often identical for pages at a time. The
differences appear to be occasioned by the demands of the dialogue form, the use of engravings of historical scenes, and an occasional effort to make the book more appealing to children. One
such attempt does not show Dunlap at his best as a historian: the
use of Dunlap's short story, "Tom Bell and the Princess Susannah
Carolina Matilda" (I, 78–88). The story is based on newspaper
accounts pieced out with conjecture, and the narrator warns us
that method is used; but he does not tell us what is fact and what
is conjecture, although he makes it somewhat clearer later in the
volume (I, 138). This is perhaps forgivable in a book intended for
young children, especially since Uncle Betterworth is remarkably
undogmatic for a textbook character. Betterworth emphasizes the
difficulty of discovering "the truth of any history" and professes
only to give his own views "having weighed the evidence which I
can find with as much critical sagacity as I possess. . . . You
must all, as you advance in your studies, read and determine for
yourselves" (II, 7).

If such humility is unusual in textbook writing, Dunlap is also
unusual for his era in the pains he takes to discourage the use of
history to provoke racial, religious, or national hatred. The preface to the first volume praises all the races which have contributed
to the history of New York. He also takes the opportunity to imply
that the Indians' behavior, although unchristian, was not unreasonable, to indicate his distaste for slavery, and to condemn extreme anti-Catholicism. He concentrates on America's struggle for
independence, but he reminds the children that one royal governor, condemned by his predecessor as a tutor-primer-writer, "was

an Englishman, an office commissioned by the King, and might think, not only that it was his duty to oppose the wishes of the people, but that it was for their good so to do" (I, 173).

Such remarks remind us that Dunlap was an unusually good man and often full of good intentions, but they do not guarantee effective textbook writing. The artificial setting imposed by the dialogue is not always sustained successfully. The children are given separate personalities with some success, but they have large vocabularies and incredibly retentive memories. After hearing about the American victory at the battle of Saratoga, John, only fourteen, asks respectfully, "Were the terms of the convention honourable to the vanquished?" (II, 189). It must not have seemed totally unrealistic dialogue in its time, or perhaps it did not matter, for Harpers reissued the book in 1855.

The textbook casts some light on the larger book it draws on: Uncle Betterworth promises the children, "At some future period I may present to you a more ambitious history of the City of New York, and its environs" (II, 268). This statement may indicate Dunlap had not yet broadened the scope of the larger work, but the "Advertisement" to the second volume speaks of both "a history of the city and its environs" and "a more comprehensive history of the State" (II, 6), so perhaps Dunlap did not distinguish between the two. He also tells us that it will be "years before its accomplishment" (II, 6), which may indicate that the volumes published in 1839-40 were rushed to the press earlier than they might have been if Dunlap had not been fatally ill and in financial straits.

The only other Dunlap history to receive separate publication is *A Narrative of the Events which Followed Bonaparte's Campaign in Russia to the Period of his Dethronement* (1814), which also appears as an appendix to Sir Robert Ker's *A Narrative of the Campaign in Russia During the Year 1812* (1814). This Dunlap book was obviously commissioned to bring an American edition up to date. Similar in character is Dunlap's "Second Part, from the Attack on the Castle of Burgos to the Taking of Bordeaux" in Francis L. Clarke's *The Life of the Most Noble Arthur, Marquis and Earl of Wellington* (1814). Both appear to be, as one admits to being, "guided principally by official dispatches" (*Wellington*, p. 369). Dunlap is, however, sensible enough to note "the usual style of European official dispatches, where exaggeration of the enemy's losses, and careful concealment of their own disasters, appear to be the main object of the writers" (*Napoleon,* p. 35). Accordingly, he makes no pretense to be anything more than current. Once again Dunlap advises that posterity must await "the future historian" who, writing after Wellington's death, can speak "from a more perfect knowledge of his private virtues and public actions than I possess" (*Wellington,* p. 422).

Both of these Dunlap books focus on military history, while displaying the author's dislike of war. Neither book is anti-French, although Dunlap favors the constitutional monarchy of England over the despotism of Napoleon. He is sympathetic to the French Revolution, which shook off "the enormous abuses of a kingly government," and believes the French were "forced into war by the interference of foreign nations in their internal regulations" (*Napoleon,* p. 137). Dunlap praises Napoleon for telling his deputies "with a rather greater mixture of truth than the rulers of Europe usually display in their communications to their subjects and the world, that he has met with great reverses of fortune and sustained great losses" (4). About the motives of England's Continental allies, Dunlap can be cynical. When he relates that the King of Prussia calls for peace and justice in Europe, Dunlap comments: "The desires of his Prussian majesty are most natural to a little despot like himself, surrounded by great ones" (133). He admires Wellington but ranks him below Marlborough and refuses "to write a panegyric" (*Wellington,* 423). Such relative objectivity is made possible by Dunlap's lack of involvement with his subject. The best we can say for these works is that they are no worse than the histories they supplement.

Dunlap's political and military histories all incur this sort of negative praise. The Napoleonic histories are competent hackwork; the history for schools is well intentioned; the one of New York is a remarkable achievement for an aged and dying man. From them we learn a bit more about Dunlap's interests and beliefs, but they are of interest because they are by Dunlap, not because they are worth reading in themselves. They add little to his achievement or to his reputation.

V *Periodical Contributions*

Many of Dunlap's contributions to periodicals were published anonymously and cannot be uncovered, but some of these have been traced through his diaries. His letters do not give much help; one particularly tantalizing letter assures a friend that in "your friend Fenno's . . . papers you will generally find some trifle of mine—You must find them out by your own sagacity." [16]

One poem from about the same time as this letter, "Ella, a Norwegian Tale," was published in the *New York Magazine* in 1791 over the signature "W. D." It can be identified certainly as Dunlap's by its later, signed appearance in his friend Smith's *American Poems* (1793).[17] The heroine of the poem, the princess of the royal house of Sweden, puts on armor and rallies the Norwegians against a treacherous attack by Sweden. In two articles, A. B. Benson has suggested possible sources for the poem, first in the *Ragnar Lodbrok Saga,* and second in a 1696 translation of Abbe Vertot's *Histoire des Revolutions des Suede* (1695).[18] The poem is an indifferent narrative ballad, of some interest as an early American use of Scandinavian materials. Perhaps the most remarkable thing about the poem is that of all Dunlap's work it should have been singled out for attention in two scholarly articles.

Another poem reprinted in Smith, "Cololoo," incorporates as a "Song" the ballad "Logan's Triumphs" published earlier in the *New-York Magazine.*[19] Like "Ella," it exploits material later used at greater length and to greater effect by greater writers. It shows, too, that Dunlap's pro-Indian views were arrived at early, part of his youthful humanitarian radicalism. Cololoo is a Noble Savage to the core, not a proto-Christian but a proud and brave warrior who curses the treacherous whites who have stolen the land. "Ella" and "Cololoo" have a crude vigor, but they do not prompt us to wish Dunlap had become as prolific a poet as he was a dramatist. The poems are not, however, out of place in Smith's volume, the first real anthology of native poetry. Some of the company is distinguished—it includes Freneau and the Connecticut Wits—but "Ella" is at least as good as the "Eulogium on Rum" by J. Smith which follows it; and "Cololoo" is far less tedious than the poem which precedes it, Theodore Dwight's "Ode to Conscience." The few poems and songs from later years that can be clearly identified as Dunlap's show no improvement over "Ella" and "Coloo." [20]

Such of Dunlap's miscellaneous essays as possess any interest have already been mentioned, save for an 1837 review of "Mr. Catlin's Lectures." [21] This essay speaks favorably of Catlin's lectures and art, once more showing Dunlap's acuity about art. More entertaining are some tales, based on Dunlap's research in New York history, that evidently aim at the tone of Washington Irving's *Sketch Book.* "Tom Bell," for example, takes place "in a village, which in the good old time was famous for witches"; the story features an eccentric schoolmaster and fraudulent magician named Ezekiel Homestriker.[22] More in the vein of the sentimental novel, "The Vanity of Human Wishes" manages in a few hundred words to encompass the ruin of two generations of a family.[23] Significantly perhaps, the beginning of it all is a father who neglects his son because he is preoccupied with making money.

Dunlap's own magazine, *The Monthly Recorder* (April–August, 1813), is dull enough to have deserved its quick death. Some of the material is later incorporated in his histories of New York and of American art. Although we cannot prove authorship, Dunlap seemingly wrote most of the magazine himself. He is almost certainly the anonymous critic of his magazine's "Dramatic Record" and is probably the author of two letters on the theater by "Timothy Teazable." The surest sign of Dunlap's hand is in a review of a production of *Abaellino,* "one of the monsters of the modern drama, which though possessing the absurdities of the German stage, is free from the contemptible weaknesses of every description which stigmatize the present English playwriters" (I, 263). The "Record" notes the play was very popular when first translated in 1801 (by Dunlap) and attributes its decline in popularity partly to "the Mohawk mutilations of would-be amenders" (I, 263). Elsewhere, the critic deplores "the immoral and sophisticated passages" in *School for Scandal* (I, 198), criticizes Cooper for playing Hotspur too much like a fine gentleman (I, 57), and promises at some time to discuss the "propriety" of modern alterations of Shakespeare. These remarks are in line with Dunlap's moralism, concern for faithful representations of life, and resistance to adaptations of Shakespeare.

Not all of Dunlap's periodical work has been uncovered, and no doubt more Dunlap items are lodged anonymously or under pseudonyms in periodicals. Those we have discussed should indicate, however, that the missing items cannot be considered a probable loss to literature. His first magazine appearances represent his youthful interest in art and ideas, but they have no real literary value. His later periodical work is mostly commercial in intent and not very good of its kind. But we can still find something to admire in his other minor works: the valuable sources preserved in his biography of Brown, the well-told anecdotes in his life of Cooke, the theater atmosphere of his novel, the unflagging energy shown in his history of New York. Circumstances forced Dunlap, like a hack, to seek commissions; but, if we add to the best of his minor works the permanent achievements of his histories of American art and American theater, then he surely deserves to be known as a man of letters. And, if that term is only a politer one for hack, Dunlap has earned our courtesy.

CHAPTER 7

The Professional

OBJECTIVELY considered, Dunlap's life was a failure. Only once was he formally declared bankrupt, but he was often on the verge of it. Having failed as a theater manager, he then failed as a magazine editor. As a painter, he repeatedly found himself unable to attract custom for any length of time in the larger cities. In his last years, plagued by illness, he spent much of his time juggling bills and notes. None of his plays has had a regular professional production in this century, and few of his paintings are on regular display. If posterity's verdict is the measure of an artist, by this measure Dunlap also seems to have been a failure.

Dunlap is well known to scholars with a special interest in the Federal period of American literature or in the history of American art or theater. The general student of American literature is often not familiar with Dunlap. In our histories and in our school curricula, American drama—at least before O'Neill—is often treated as if it were not quite literature, although it is a strange definition of literature that can encompass sermons, letters, lectures, and editorials, to say nothing of the poetry of Michael Wigglesworth or Timothy Dwight, and yet find no place for drama. Since Dunlap's chief contributions to our literature were made as a dramatist, it is possible that he has received less general recognition than he merits.

Dunlap was not a Shakespeare—not even a Sheridan or a Kotzebue. He knew as much himself, and in his *History of the American Theatre* he does not attempt to conceal his limitations from the reader. He knew, too, what claim upon posterity's attention he might make: in the major histories and in his biography of Brown he praises the generation of pioneers who sought to answer the call for an indigenous American art, and he surely realized he belonged in their company. To point to an artist's historical importance is often to confess that he lacks literary value. But there are at least two classes of artists whom we value for their historical importance, and Dunlap falls in the second and more worthy of these. In the first class is the author whose work is inferior even in his own day but who is nonetheless extremely popular and even influential. For example, Margaret Mitchell's *Gone With the Wind* is not the novel of the Civil War that William Faulkner's *Absalom, Absalom!* is, but it will be grist for the mill of future literary historians. In the second class is the author whose work lacks the enduring appeal of a classic but is superior in its time and place. The early literary history of most nations is full of such figures; in fact, early American literary history would scarcely exist if we excluded them, and Dunlap belongs in their number.

When measured against his contemporaries in American drama, Dunlap fairs well. Tyler's *The Contrast* is a better play than any of Dunlap's surviving comedies; but, in the period in which Dunlap wrote most of his plays, no other American matched him in comedy. In tragedy and the Gothic play, in translations and adaptations, he had no rival in this period. If we allow for changing theatrical conditions (which give the illusion of progress), Dunlap's plays have as much right to serious attention as those of such later figures as Augustin Daly, David Belasco, Clyde Fitch, and Augustus Thomas, and our own day could no doubt provide other examples. Even those who measure our drama by the standard of England should not find Dunlap disgraced when placed beside his immediate English contemporaries. The later Richard Brinsley Sheridan, George Colman, Mrs. Inchbald, and John O'Keeffe may be superior to Dunlap; but they by no means dwarf him.

Dunlap's contemporaries in other branches of our literature have no stronger claim on posterity than he. In the novel, William Hill Brown's *The Power of Sympathy* and Susanna Rowson's *Charlotte Temple* exploit sentimental effects at greater length but with no greater merit than do many Dunlap plays. *André* and one or two other plays are clearly superior to our first novels. Dunlap's friend Brown's novels range from better than anything of Dunlap's to worse than anything of Dunlap's. The few fine lyrics or lyric passages by Freneau or the Hartford Wits do not offset the mediocre quality of the bulk of their work. Joel Barlow is in many ways the best of the latter group; but, unlike Dunlap, he is least effective when he applies himself most seriously. For every person who can now read Barlow's *The Columbiad* with pleasure, there must be many who could read any number of Dunlap plays with pleasure. As a dramatist, Dunlap deserves a place in our sense of our literary heritage.

Like those of his contemporaries, Dunlap's plays are marked by an emphasis on sentimentality at the expense of action. The most important personal characteristic they display is an interest in situations bearing on the relationship of fathers and sons. Obvious in *The Father* and *Ribbemont,* the relationship is suggested in several other plays, notably *André* and *Leicester.* The same interest finds expression in several ways in Dunlap's one novel. The pattern of rebellion and guilt has obvious autobiographical roots, but the surviving letters and diaries do not permit us to say how deep they go.

In *André,* the theme of guilt and rebellion is tied to the Revolution; Dunlap's best play is thus the result of a natural fit between Dunlap's psychic concerns and the cultural dilemma of the new republic. Dunlap touches on this theme in a number of plays, and it is of course important to our understanding of his major histories. Dunlap's artistic career also illustrates the problems his generation faced. It was easier for Dunlap to be an adapter of English plays than a writer of American plays. Even when the work was his own, he found it more profitable to present it as an English play or an English translation of a Continental drama.

Given the unnatural situations and stock characters of the plays, Dunlap's dialogue is often remarkably natural. His blank verse uses the inverted syntax of its tradition but generally avoids stilted, self-consciously poetic diction. The homely likenesses of his portraits show up in the plays in this way, although the actions required by his plots rarely allow his stage characters the reality we sense in the paintings. Dunlap's own criterion of naturalness is best met by the anecdotal portraits of his histories, where he is free from worrying about the plot devices audiences like and the parts actors like. A few of the characters in his novel have the same three-dimensional quality, perhaps because he was writing from his own memories of the theater.

Dunlap himself is one of the most agreeable of the characters we encounter in the histories—and one of their chief attractions. Dunlap the man has a full assortment of faults: he is vain even when being modest; he is sometimes unfair to those he thinks

have wronged him or too kind to his friends; he is always garrulous; but he seemed to many of his contemporaries peculiarly lovable. He is rarely bitter about the unpleasant experiences, the
sickness, the failure that marked his career, and he seldom shows
self-pity. Not blind to the weaknesses of his friends, he is loyal to
a fault; hardly all-forgiving, he is still willing to see merit in those
who have been his enemies. Useful in the histories, these qualities
made it possible for him to write them, just as in life they enabled
him to retain so many friends and make so few enemies.

Dunlap deserves our gratitude for the memorials he left to his
generation and his friends, and he deserves some credit for the
wide range of interests they reflect. For a time, he was the leading
dramatist of the American theater; later, he was its best historian.
He was one of the new republic's first generation of painters and
their best historian. His biography of Brown contains source material that might otherwise have been lost. His novel and the life
of Cooke give us additional glimpses into the artistic world of the
early nineteenth century. His political histories and miscellaneous
work have no such merits, but they indicate the continued seriousness of his ambition. And it is by his total achievement that he
must be judged.

In becoming a bankrupt artist, Dunlap changed from an amateur dabbler in the arts to a thoroughgoing professional. As a
critic, he foresaw that America's commercial society would make a
trade of art; as an artist, he did his best to make art a respectable
trade. Greater artists were to come, but America owes much to
her first generation of professionals. If we remember those who
made a place for art in America, William Dunlap will not be forgotten.

Notes and References

Chapter One

1. The analogy has been developed at length by Seymour Lipset in *The First New Nation* (New York, 1963), pp. 13–98.

2. Dunlap, *History of the Rise and Progress of the Arts of Design in the United States* (2 vols.; New York, 1834), I, 243—hereafter cited as *Arts*. The *History of the American Theatre* is cited (as *Theatre*) from the expanded two-volume edition (London, 1833), which is evidently the text used for a recent reprint (New York, 1963). Another important source is the three-volume "Diary of William Dunlap," *Collections of the New York Historical Society*, LXII–LXIV (1929–31), cited as *Diary*. These are also the basic sources for the biographical portions of two other books used in this chapter: an unpublished dissertation (Wisconsin, 1946) by Charles W. Getchell, "The Mind and Art of William Dunlap (1766–1839)," and Oral Sumner Coad, *William Dunlap* (New York, 1917), reprinted (New York, 1962). Some diaries unavailable to Coad earlier are dealt with in Coad, "The Dunlap Diaries at Yale," *Studies in Philology*, XXIV (1924), 402–12. References to "Coad" in the text and notes are to the biography unless otherwise noted.

3. Coad, p. 22, places the change in early 1790.

4. See Mary Rives Bowman, "Dunlap and the 'Theatrical Register' of the *New York Magazine*," *Studies in Philology* XXIV (1924), 413–25, for this identification.

5. V. L. Parrington, *Main Currents in American Thought* (New York, 1927–30), I, 361.

6. William Johnson, in a joint letter with Smith and Brown to Dunlap, recorded in *Diary*, I, 336.

7. In a letter in 1847, quoted in James E. Cronin, "Elihu Hubbard Smith and the New York Friendly Club, 1795–1798," *PMLA*, LXIV (1949), 474.

8. "Remarks on the Love of Country," *New York Magazine*, n.s. II (1797), 582–84. Godwin's undated reply to Dunlap's letter is in the manuscript collection of the Historical Society of Pennsylvania—hereafter cited as "PHi." Also there is a letter to Dunlap from God-

win's friend Thomas Holcroft, January 20, 1796, wishing well to Dunlap and his "associates."

9. Alan S. Downer, ed., *The Memoir of John Durang: American Actor, 1785–1816* (Pittsburgh, 1966), pp. 31–32.

10. Smith, letter to Dr. Mason F. Cogswell, March 12, 1795, in Beindecke Rare Book and Manuscript Library, Yale.

11. *Theatre*, II, 214, cited from a diary volume now lost.

12. Coad, p. 81. George C. D. Odell, *Annals of the New York Stage* (15 vols.; New York, 1927–49), II, 219–26, has a similar evaluation, but cf. George O. Seilhamer, *History of the American Theatre* (3 vols,; Philadelphia, 1888–91), III, 387.

13. Winslow Ames, in Phillips Academy, *William Dunlap, Painter and Critic* (Andover, Mass., 1939), p. 8. For a recent study of the conditions Dunlap faced, see Neil Harris, *The Artist in American Society: The Formative Years, 1790–1860* (New York, 1966). On intinerancy, see especially pp. 69–73.

14. Getting a discouraging reply from Gulian C. Verplanck, letter to Dunlap, January 29, 1829, at PHi.

15. Letter to Robert Gilmore, January 7, 1832, asks his help— cited from David McNeely Stauffer, *Westcott's History of Philadelphia* (Philadelphia, 1913), at PHi.

16. Letter to James Fenimore Cooper, September 20, 1831, at Yale. Unless otherwise indicated, all letters from William Dunlap or John Dunlap to Cooper are cited from the Yale Cooper papers. This letter is reprinted in the *Correspondence of James Fenimore Cooper*, Vol. I (New Haven, 1922), pp. 240–45.

17. *New York Mirror*, X (February 23, 1833), 266.

18. Oral S. Coad, "William Dunlap, New Jersey Artist," *Proceedings of the New Jersey Historical Society*, LXXXIII (1965), 238–63. For evaluations of his painting, see also Virgil Barker, *American Painting* (New York, 1950), p. 334; James Thomas Flexner, *The Light of Distant Skies, American Painting, 1760–1835* (New York, 1945), p. 165; E. P. Richardson, *Painting in America* (New York, 1965), pp. 79–80; Samuel Isham, *History of American Painting* (rev. ed.; New York, 1927), pp. 72–79. The Ames pamphlet cited above in note 13 is for a centennial exhibition of paintings by Dunlap and painters mentioned in the *Arts*. The reviews of the exhibition give an idea of Dunlap's standing: "American Vasari," *Magazine of Art*, XXXII (1939), 592–94; "*Andover:* William Dunlap, Painter and Critic," *Art News*, XXXVIII (October 7, 1939), 13; "Dunlap, the 'American Vasari' and His Age," *Art Digest*, XIV (October 1, 1939), 10; Jane T. Johnson, "William Dunlap and His Times," *Antiques*, XXXVII (February, 1940), 72–74. For an unfavorable evaluation of Dunlap's work in the

genre, see Harry B. Wehle, *American Miniatures, 1730–1850* (Garden City, 1927), pp. 52, 53.

19. Coad, "William Dunlap, New Jersey Artist," p. 254.

20. Letter to James Fenimore Cooper, April 4, 1837.

21. *New York Mirror*, X (February 23, 1833), 265.

22. Dunlap, *The Life of Charles Brockden Brown* (2 vols.; Philadelphia, 1815), II, 10—hereafter cited as *Brown*.

23. Brown, letter to Dunlap, January 1, 1798, at PHi.

24. Smith, letter to Dunlap, July 29, 1797, at PHi.

25. Getchell, pp. 84–121, discusses Dunlap's religious ideas.

26. Letter to James Fenimore Cooper, September, 1831.

27. *Ibid.*

28. Letter to James Fenimore Cooper, December 28, 1832, cited from *Correspondence of James Fenimore Cooper*, I, 305–7.

29. Letter to James Fenimore Cooper, June 16, 1836.

30. See Marvin Meyer's analysis in *The Jacksonian Persuasion* (Stanford, 1957), pp. 45–55.

31. Brown, letter to Dunlap, February 25, 1805, at PHi. Reprinted in *Brown*, II, 112–13, with minor variants.

32. Letter to Robert Weir, September 27, 1834, at University of Virginia Library.

33. Or at least the careful work of engraving—Letter to John G. Chapman, January 11, 1839, at University of Virginia.

34. Dunlap, "Charles Brockden Brown," *National Portrait Gallery*, ed. James Herring and James R. Longacre, III (New York, 1836), no page number given.

35. James Fenimore Cooper, letter to Mrs. Cooper, June 1, 1936, cited from *Letters and Journals of James Fenimore Cooper*, ed. James Franklin Beard, II (Cambridge, 1964), 224. Also in *Correspondence of James Fenimore Cooper*, I, 362.

36. Letter to James Fenimore Cooper, October 1, 1836.

37. Letter to James Fenimore Cooper, March 14, 1837.

38. Letter to James Fenimore Cooper, March 18, 1837.

39. Letter to James Fenimore Cooper, April 21, 1837; letter to James Fenimore Cooper, June 12, 1837.

40. The estimated date is based on John A. Dunlap, letter to James Fenimore Cooper, October 4, 1839, the first of a series of letters.

41. *Ibid.*

Chapter Two

1. Letter to James Fenimore Cooper, July 24, 1833.

2. Letters to George Bancroft, March 5, 1835, and May 5, 1835, at Massachusetts Historical Society. Quote from first.

3. But on Quidor cf. Barker, *American Painting*, pp. 496–501.

4. Dunlap inquires after a recently sent packet of autographs and asks for information about a Baltimore painter in a letter to Robert Gilmore, July 15, 1833, at PHi.

5. Note by Cole on the bottom of a Dunlap letter to Cole, August 28, 1834, at New York State Library, Albany.

6. Sargent, letter to Dunlap, May 5, 1833.

7. Allston, letter to Dunlap, April 6, 1833 (*Diary*, III, 672–73).

8. Letter to [James McMurtie?], May 11, 1833, at PHi.

9. Letter to Henry Inman, December 20, 1833, at PHi.

10. Letter to Joseph B. Boyd, another autograph collector, September 12, 1837, at PHi.

11. Letter to Matthew Carey, December 20, 1832, at PHi; Letter to George Bancroft, May 27, 1835, at Massachusetts Historical Society.

12. Letter to James Rees, March 13, 1838, at Boston Public Library.

13. Letter to Robert Gilmore, December 17, 1832, at PHi.

14. Letter to James Rees, March 13, 1838, at Boston Public Library.

15. *Review of the "Biographical Sketch" of John Vanderlyn published by William Dunlap in his "History of the Arts of Design": with some additional notices respecting Mr. Vanderlyn, As an Artist. By a friend of the artist* (New York, 1838), p. 62, by the author of "a memoir written by a friend of the artist" (*Arts*, II, 31) used in the history. It may be Vanderlyn himself, whom Dunlap asked for information (*Diary*, III, 743) and who gave some (*Diary*, III, 806, 813, 824).

16. For specific inaccuracies, see: H. E. Dickson, "A Misdated Episode in Dunlap," *Art Quarterly*, IX (1946), 33–36; Anna Wells Rutledge, "Dunlap Notes," *Art in America*, XXXIX (1951), 36–48. For over-all evaluations of the *Arts*, see the exhibition pamphlet and reviews cited in n. 18 to Chapter II and the following general treatments: Flexner, p. 68; Isham, p. 72; Richardson, p. 161; Suzanne LaFollete, *Art in America* (New York, 1929), pp. 73–74; and Oliver W. Larkin, *Art and Life in America* (New York, 1949), p. 153. On the *Theatre*: Seilhamer, II, 274, is harshly unfavorable, although Seilhamer uses the *Theatre* often; Mary Caroline Crawford, *The Romance of the American Theater* (Boston, 1913), p. 97n., defends Dunlap against Seilhamer. Also friendly is Arthur Hobson Quinn, *History of the American Drama, from the Beginning to the Civil War*, 2nd ed. (New York, 1943), p. 75. All critics commenting on the *Arts* seem friendly. Received too late for use in this study were: Harold E. Dickson, *Arts of the Young Republic: The Age of William Dunlap* (Chapel Hill, 1968) and David Grimsted *Melodrama Unveiled: American Theater and Culture, 1800–1850* (Chicago, 1968).

17. Letter to James Fenimore Cooper, September 20, 1831. This letter probably refers to a similar project, a periodical "to give a view of the fine arts in every part of the world—their history & that of their professors"—letter to James Fenimore Cooper, June 15, 1831.

18. The history of this theme in American literary criticism is well told in Benjamin T. Spencer, *The Quest for Nationality, an American Literary Campaign* (Syracuse, 1957). On the fine arts, see Harris, *Artist in American Society,* and Lillian B. Miller, *Patrons and Patriotism, the Encouragement of the Fine Arts in the United States, 1790–1860* (Chicago, 1966).

19. Dunlap, *Address to the Students of the National Academy* (New York, 1831), p. 11—hereafter cited in text as *Address:* Elihu Hubbard Smith, ed., *American Poems, Selected and Original* (Litchfield, Conn., 1793).

20. See Miller, *Patrons and Patriotism,* pp. 90–102, for a more objective account of the dispute between the Academies and some discussion of the artists' resentment of "patronage."

21. Letter to Robert Gilmore, February 28, 1835, at Boston Public Library.

22. See Van Carl Kussrow, "On with the Show, a Study of Public Arguments in Favor of Theatre in America During the Eighteenth Century," unpublished dissertation (Indiana, 1959).

23. Royall Tyler, "Preface," *The Algerine Captive* (2 vols.; Hartford, 1816), I, vi.

24. *Thirty Years Ago; or, the Memoirs of a Water-Drinker* (2 vols.; New York, 1836), I, vi.—Hereafter cited as *Water-Drinker.*

25. Cf. Philadelphia manager William Wood, *Personal Recollections of the Stage* (Philadelphia, 1855). Fred Moramarco, "The Early Dramatic Criticism of William Dunlap," *American Literature,* XL (1968), 9–14, suggests that some of the "Theatrical Register" essays mark a shift from moral to esthetic criteria (realism), citing the author's disapproval of Nahum Tate's eighteenth-century version of *Lear.* This would seem to be less a shift than an early example of Dunlap's ability to distinguish moral from esthetic criteria. We may also note that Tate's *Lear* has more sexual "immorality" than the original.

26. Letter to R. Penn Smith *et al.,* December 11, 1837, at PHi, declining an invitation to a banquet for Edwin Forrest, but offering a toast.

27. Letter to [James McMurtie], May 11, 1833, at PHi.

28. Reynolds, *Discourses on Art,* ed. Robert E. Wark (San Marino Cal., 1959), pp. 100, 101 (Sixth discourse). Cf. pp. 41–47 (Third discourse) for denigration of Nature in the raw.

29. Flexner, pp. 74–76.

30. Dunlap, "Gilbert Stuart," *National Portrait Gallery*, ed. Herring and Longacre, Vol. I (New York, 834), no page number given.

31. Exhibition review, *Art Digest*, XIV (October 1, 1939), 10.

32. Letter to Robert Gilmore, February 28, 1835, at Boston Public Library.

33. *North American Magazine*, II (1833), 263–64. Checking on Dunlap's criticism is made more difficult by the lack of scholarly studies in this field. Garff B. Wilson's excellent *A History of American Acting* (Bloomington, 1966) begins with Edwin Forrest and his school.

34. Exhibition review, *Art News*, XXXVIII (October 7, 1939), 13.

Chapter Three

1. *Theatre*, I, 147. On the resemblance, see Coad, p. 137, and Quinn, p. 75.

2. *The Father of an Only Child* (New York, 1807), p. 3, the edition used in the text. References to the original are to *The Father* (New York, 1789).

3. *Darby's Return* (New York, 1789), the edition used in the text; omissions are indicated by inverted commas.

4. *Yankee Chronology* (New York, 1812), p. 12n., the edition used in the text.

5. *Theatre*, II, 280, dismisses it in a sentence; Coad, p. 177; Quinn, p. 107.

6. *A Trip to Niagara* (New York, 1830), p. 3, the edition used in the text.

7. Frederick Bond, *The Negro and the Drama* (Washington, 1940), p. 21.

8. Bond, pp. 21–22. See Bond, pp. 21–34, for a survey of some early appearances of the Negro in American drama. For other Yankee plays, consult Francis Hodge, *Yankee Theatre* (Austin, 1964), which suggests (p. 162) that Dunlap's play may have been influenced by his contact with the English comedian Charles Matthews, whose satirical sketch, *A Trip to America* (1824) influenced many later Yankee plays. Kent G. Gallagher, *The Foreigner in Early American Drama* (The Hague, 1966) gives useful summaries of American plays dealing with foreigners, including several of Dunlap's.

9. Smith's diary, quoted in Cronin, "Smith and the New York Friendly Club," *PMLA*, LXIV (1949), 478.

10. Coad, p. 150; Quinn, p. 80.

11. Odell, II, 49, quotes a review in the *New York Commercial Advertiser*, February 11, 1799.

12. Odell, II, 103, quoting a December 6, 1800 review, which is apparently from the *Commercial Advertiser*.

13. Odell, II, 195, quotes a review of March 2, 1804, apparently from the *New York Morning Chronicle.*

Chapter Four

1. *Leicester* (New York, 1807), p. [3], the edition used in the text; *Theatre*, I, 207.

2. Coad, pp. 144–45, points out other *Macbeth* parallels.

3. Odell, II, 170, quoting the *New York Morning Chronicle*, February 3, 1803.

4. *Ribbemont; or, The Feudal Baron* (New York, 1803), is the edition used in the text.

5. Hodgkinson, *The Man of Fortitude; or, The Knight's Adventure* (New York, 1807), the edition used in the text.

6. *André* (New York, 1798), p. iii, the edition used in the text.

7. William Alfred Bryan, *George Washington in American Literature, 1775–1865* (New York, 1952), p. 179n. But Dunlap, if the author of the "Theatrical Register" essays, had not too long since registered some objections to the Otway play—cited in Moramarco, "The Early Dramatic Criticism of William Dunlap," p. 13.

8. But in Act I, Scene 2, it is Seward who hopes America's example may help other nations "reassume the dignity of man" and M'Donald who is unsure whether other nations will be as able to "submit to Order's gentle voice" once having broken "Coercion's iron yoke." The clash is between Seward's nativist idealism and M'Donald's reasoned sense of history. The passing reference implied here to the French Revolution may be taken as evidence of Federalism or as a common-sense statement.

9. Bryan, p. 179; Quinn, p. 87.

10. Some cuts are indicated in the printing of *The Glory of Columbia—Her Yeomanry* (New York, 1817), the edition used in the text. Still other cuts were evidently made in performance.

Chapter Five

1. *Fontainville Abbey* (New York, 1807), p. [153], the edition used in the text. This edition is made up of separate sheets from the first volume of his collected plays.

2. Coad, p. 153, also believes Dunlap knew Boaden's play, although the only evidence he cites is the use of Hortensia as Madame LaMotte's name—she is Constance in the book. The name he could have taken from an English playbill—as a translator, he sometimes uses names from British translations to appeal to his audience's Anglophile prejudices. But the weight of the evidence, given in the text, suggests that he had read Boaden.

3. *The Archers; or, Mountaineers of Switzerland* (New York, 1796), p. v, the edition used in the text.

4. *The Italian Father* (New York, 1810), p. [3], the edition used in the text. Richard Penn Smith later used both Dekker and Dunlap for his *The Deformed* (1830)—Bruce Welker McCullough, *The Life and Writings of Richard Penn Smith* (Menasha, Wis., 1917), p. 17, a University of Pennsylvania dissertation. McCullough reprints the Smith play.

5. Of the editions listed in the Blanck bibliography, those of Boaden's *Maid of Bristol* (New York, 1803), Colman's *Blue Beard* (New York, 1802), and Prince Hoare's *Chains of the Heart* (New York, 1804), fall in this category. Dunlap's role cannot be estimated in *Barnaby Brittle, Altered from Molière and Betterton's Wanton Wife* (New York, 1806), which notes it has been "Altered by William Dunlap, J. H. Payne, and others."

6. Myron Matlow, "Some Kotzebue Plays in England and America: *The Stranger* and *Pizarro*," unpublished dissertation (Chicago, 1953), p. 44. Matlow, p. 49, says Dunlap probably did publish his version.

7. These include *The School for Soldiers* (1799) from Mercier's *Le Déserteur*, *The Robbery* (1799) from de Monvel's *Clementine et Désormes*, *Abbé de l'Épée* (1801) from Bouily, and *Nina* (1804) from Marsollier's opera.

Chapter Six

1. Brown, letter to Dunlap, February 25, 1805, at PHi. Reprinted in *Brown*, II, 112–13, with minor variations in wording.

2. Edward H. O'Neill, *A History of American Biography* (Philadelphia, 1935), p. 24.

3. *Ibid.*; Ernest Marchand, "The Literary Opinions of Charles Brockden Brown," *Studies in Philology*, XXXI (1934), 562.

4. Paul Allen, letter to Dunlap, July 8, 1814, at PHi.

5. Donald A. Ringe, *Charles Brockden Brown* (New York, 1966), p. 153.

6. Marchand, p. 546.

7. Wood, *Personal Recollections*, p. 158.

8. Lamb is quoted by Allston, letter to Dunlap, April 6, 1833 (*Diary*, III, 673); Byron is quoted in Crawford, *Romance of the American Theatre*, p. 97.

9. O'Neill, p. 25; see also Van Wyck Brooks, *The World of Washington Irving* (New York, 1944), p. 171.

10. Godwin, letter to Dunlap, undated, at PHi.

11. Letter to James Fenimore Cooper, August 12, 1836.

12. Brooks, p. 171.

13. Letter to James Fenimore Cooper, August 12, 1836.

14. Letter to John G. Chapman, January 11, 1839, at the University of Virginia.

15. Robin Brooks, "Alexander Hamilton, Melancton Smith, and the Ratification of the Constitution in New York," *William & Mary Quarterly*, XXIV (1967), 341–42, shows that Dunlap's history (II, 281n.) contains a reminiscence by a convention attender which has served as the eventual source for several modern historians. Unfortunately, the reminiscence seems to be incorrect. James H. Pickering, "*Satanstoe*: Cooper's Debt to William Dunlap," *American Literature*, XXXVIII (1967), 468–77, discusses Cooper's unacknowledged debt in this novel to the New York history and to other Dunlap works.

16. Letter to Mason [F. Cogswell], March, 1790, at Yale.

17. *New-York Magazine*, II (1791), 235–36; Smith, pp. 226–31.

18. Adolph B. Benson, "Scandinavian Influences in the Works of William Dunlap and Richard Alsop," *Scandinavian Studies and Notes*, IX (1927), 239–57, and "The Sources of William Dunlap's *Ella, a Norwegian Tale*," *Scandinavian Studies*, XIX (1946), 136–43.

19. Smith, pp. 287–91; *New-York Magazine*, II (1791), 52–53, signed "W. D." Since this chapter was written, Lewis Leary has noted the magazine publication of "Ella" and "Logan's Triumphs"—"Unrecorded Early Verse by William Dunlap," *American Literature*, XXXIX (1967), 87–88. Leary points out that this makes Dunlap probably the author of "A Passage from Dante thrown into English heroic Verse," *New-York Magazine*, II (1791) also signed "W. D." and important as the first appearance of Dante in American literature.

Leary lists four poems signed "D." from the same magazine and possibly by Dunlap: "Ode for the New Year," I (1790), 52; "Elegy on a Broken Flute," I (1790), 172–73; "A Reflection," II (1791), 441; and "Elegiac Ode," III (1792), 504–5. The first of these bids farewell to "blest Eighty-Nine," which would have special meaning for Dunlap, for whom 1789 was not merely the year of the new government but the year of his marriage, his first stage successes, and his first child.

20. Jacob Blanck, ed., *Bibliography of American Literature*, II (New Haven, 1957), 506–18, is the standard Dunlap bibliography. The separately published songs it lists include several from plays and one or two others apparently written to be sung between acts. They range from sentimental songs to noisy patriotic numbers. Dunlap contributed two translations of Gesner poems to the *New-York Magazine* in 1795 and 1796 (VI, 760; n.s. I, 49). Their broken English renderings show that Dunlap was not yet the master of German. Much improvement is seen in "The Dancing Bear," taken from Gellert and

published some years after it was written in the *New York Mirror,* XV (July 8, 1837), 10.

21. *New York Mirror,* XV (October 14, 1837), 126.
22. *New York Mirror,* XIV (November 12, 1836), 157–58.
23. *New York Mirror,* XV (November 30, 1837), 211.

Selected Bibliography

PRIMARY SOURCES

This listing is based on the Blanck bibliography and on the bibliography in the Coad biography. I have left out adaptations which do not significantly alter the original and reprints of songs from plays. In the case of translations, the original author's name is indicated in parentheses before the title entry. Dunlap's plays were sometimes reissued with new title pages; I have used some of these editions in the text, but I have tried to list only the important new editions. The most convenient source for most Dunlap plays is the *Three Centuries of Drama* series put out by Readex Microprint. It should, however, be checked against the Blanck bibliography as it contains a number of doubtful attributions.

1. *Separate Publications*

The Father; or, American Shandyism. New York: Hodge, Allen & Campbell, 1789.

Darby's Return. New York: Hodge, Allen, and Campbell, 1789.

The Archers; or, Mountaineers of Switzerland. New York: T. & J. Swords, 1796.

(Robineau) *Tell Truth and Shame the Devil.* New York: T. & J. Swords, 1797.

André. New York: T. & J. Swords, 1798.

(Kotzebue) *The Wild Goose Chace.* New York: for the author, 1800.

(Kotzebue) *The Virgin of the Sun.* New York: for the author, 1800.

(Kotzebue) *Pizarro in Peru; or, The Death of Rolla.* New York: for the author, 1800.

(Zschokke) *Abaellino, the Great Bandit.* New York: D. Longworth, 1802.

Ribbemont; or, The Feudal Baron. New York: D. Longworth, 1803.

(Caigniez) *The Voice of Nature.* New York: David Longworth, 1803.

(Pixerécourt) *The Wife of Two Husbands.* New York: D. Longworth, 1804.

The Dramatic Works of William Dunlap. Vol. I. Philadelphia: T. and G. Palmer, 1806. (Includes *The Father of an Only Child, Darby's*

Return, Fontainville Abbey, and Leicester. All were reissued separately in 1807 by Longworth.)

The Man of Fortitude; or, the Knight's Adventure. New York: David Longworth, 1807. (As "Written by the Late John Hodgkinson.")

(Kotzebue) Fraternal Discord. New York: D. Longworth, 1809.

The Italian Father. New York: D. Longworth, 1810.

Yankee Chronology; or, Huzza for the Constitution! New York: D. Longworth, 1812.

Memoirs of the Life of George Frederick Cooke. New York: D. Longworth, 1813. Rev. ed., as The Life of George Fred. Cooke. London: Henry Colburn, 1815.

A Record, Literary and Political, of Five Months in the Year 1813. New York: David Carlisle, n.d. (Binds together issues of Dunlap's Monthly Recorder.)

(Kotzebue) Lover's Vows. New York: David Longworth, 1814.

(Iffland) The Good Neighbour. New York: David Longworth, 1814.

A Narrative of the Events Which Followed Bonaparte's Campaign in Russia to the Period of his Dethronement. Hartford: George Sheldon, 1814. (Simultaneously published as an appendix to Sir Robert Ker, A Narrative of the Campaign in Russia, during the Year 1812.)

The Life of Charles Brockden Brown. Philadelphia: James P. Parke, 1815. Reprinted, London: Henry Colburn, 1822.

A Trip to Niagara; or, Travellers in America. New York: E. B. Clayton, 1830.

Address to the Students of the National Academy of Design, at the Delivery of the Premiums. New York: Clayton & Van Norden, 1831.

A History of the American Theatre. New York: J. & J. Harper, 1832. Two-volume edition; London: Richard Bentley, 1833. Reissued, two-volumes in one, New York: Burt Franklin, 1963.

History of the Rise and Progress of the Arts of Design in the United States. 2 vols. New York: George P. Scott, 1834.

Thirty Years Ago; or, The Memoirs of a Water-Drinker. 2 vols. New York: Bancroft & Holley, 1836.

A History of New York, for Schools. 2 vols. New York: Collins, Keese, & Co.

History of the New Netherlands, Province of New York, and State of New York, to the Adoption of the Federal Constitution. 2 vols. New York: for the author, 1839–40.

Diary of William Dunlap. Ed. Dorothy C. Barck. 3 vols. New York: New York Historical Society, 1930. (Collections of the New York Historical Society, LXII–LXIV [1929–31].)

False Shame and Thirty Years. Ed. Oral Sumner Coad. Princeton: Princeton University Press, 1940. (Vol. II, *America's Lost Plays*.)

2. Other Dunlap Publications

"Logan's Triumphs." *New York Magazine; or, Literary Repository*, II (1791), 52–53.

"Ella, a Norwegian Tale." *New York Magazine; or, Literary Repository*, II (1791), 235–38.

"Ella, a Norwegian Tale" and "Cololoo." *American Poems, Selected and Original*. Ed. Elihu Hubbard Smith. Litchfield, Conn.: Collier and Buel, 1793. Pp. 226–31, 287–91.

(Gesner) "The Zephyrs, an Idyl." *New York Magazine; or, Literary Repository*, VI (1795), 760.

(Gesner) "First Idyl of Gesner." *New York Magazine; or, Literary Repository*, n.s. I (1796), 49.

"On Innocence and Generosity." *New York Magazine; or, Literary Repository*, n.s. II (1797), 518.

"Remarks on the Love of Country." *New York Magazine; or, Literary Repository*, n.s. II (1797), 582–84.

"The Second Part, from the Attack on the Castle of Burgos to the Taking of Bordeaux." Francis L. Clarke, *The Life of the Most Noble Arthur, Marquis and Earl of Wellington*. New York: Van Winkle and Wiley, 1814. Pp. 369–423.

"Biographical Sketch of the Late Gilbert Stuart." *Knickerbocker*, I (1833), 195.

"Gilbert Charles Stuart" and "Charles Brockden Brown." *National Portrait Gallery of Americans*. Ed. James Herring and James B. Longacre. New York: for the authors, 1834–39. Vol. I, no page numbers; Vol. III, no page numbers.

"Scraps and Miscellanies." *Knickerbocker*, I (1833), 195.

"Boswell's Life of Johnson." *New York Mirror*, XI (1833), 82.

"English Travellers." *New York Mirror*, XI (1833), 111.

"Memoir of Thomas Abthorpe Cooper." *New York Mirror*, XI (1833), 225.

"The Ghost Murderer." *New York Mirror*, XII (1935), 225.

"Essay on the Influence of the Arts of Design." *American Monthly Magazine*, VII (1836), 113.

"Critical Hints." *American Monthly Magazine*, VII (1836), 502.

"Tom Bell." *New York Mirror*, XIV (1836), 157.

"Tom Bell and the Princess Susannah Carolina Matilda." *New York Mirror*, XIV (1837), 217.

"The Night-Jumpers; or, The Yankee Tom and Jerry." *New York Mirror*, XV (1837), 2.

(Gellert) "The Dancing Bear." *New York Mirror,* XV (1837), 10.
"Mr. Catlin's Lectures." *New York Mirror,* XV (1837), 126.
"The Vanity of Human Wishes." *New York Mirror,* XV (1837), 211.

SECONDARY SOURCES

Only the most significant discussions of Dunlap's work are included,
but some briefer Dunlap items are listed in the Notes and References.
Anyone needing a more complete bibliography should remember to
consult the *Art Index,* as well as the standard literary bibliographies.

BENSON, ADOLPH B. "Scandinavian Influences in the works of William
    Dunlap and Richard Alsop," *Scandinavian Studies and Notes,*
    IX (1927), 239–57. Argues for a Scandinavian source for Dun-
    lap's "Ella, a Norwegian Tale." Lacks external evidence; internal
    evidence is weak.

———. "The Sources of William Dunlap's *Ella, a Norwegian Tale,*
    "*Scandinavian Studies,* XIX (1946), 136–43. Presents a new
    source for "Ella"; attribution still weak.

BLANCK, JACOB, ed. "William Dunlap." *Bibliography of American
    Literature.* Vol. II. New Haven: Yale, 1957. Pp. 506–18. Most
    reliable bibliography of Dunlap's works. Eliminates a number of
    false attributions.

BOWMAN, MARY RIVES. "Dunlap and the 'Theatrical Register' of the
    New York Magazine," *Studies in Philology,* XXIV (1924), 413–
    25. Well-argued identification of Dunlap as the magazine's anony-
    mous theater critic.

BROOKS, VAN WYCK. *The World of Washington Irving.* New York:
    E. P. Dutton, 1944. Painless presentation of Dunlap's background,
    with a chapter on "William Dunlap and his Circle" (119–37).

CANARY, ROBERT H. "William Dunlap and the Search for an American
    Audience," *Midcontinent American Studies Journal,* IV (1963),
    45–51. Brief discussion of Dunlap as a critic, covers much the
    same ground as part of Chapter II.

COAD, ORAL SUMNER. "The Dunlap Diaries at Yale," *Studies in Phil-
    ology,* XXIV (1927), 403–12. Discusses new biographical details
    revealed by diaries previously unavailable.

———. *William Dunlap.* New York: The Dunlap Society, 1917. Re-
    printed, New York: Russell & Russell, 1962. Has the most de-
    tailed biography and competent criticism. Must be consulted by
    anyone interested in Dunlap.

———. "William Dunlap, New Jersey Artist," *Proceedings of the
    New Jersey Historical Society,* LXXXIII (1965), 238–63. In-
    cludes an especially useful listing of Dunlap paintings owned by
    institutions open to the public.

DICKSON, H. E. "A Misdated Episode in Dunlap," *Art Quarterly*, IX (1946), 33–36. Corrects the art history.

———. *Arts of the Young Republic: The Age of William Dunlap*. Chapel Hill: University of North Carolina. 1968. Extensively illustrated brief discussion of Dunlap's contemporaries in painting and sculpture, as seen through his eyes.

GETCHELL, CHARLES M. "The Mind and Art of William Dunlap (1766–1839)." Unpublished Ph.D. dissertation, University of Wisconsin, 1946. Most useful for its accurate summaries of Dunlap's expressed beliefs.

GRIMSTED, DAVID. *Melodrama Unveiled: American Theater and Culture, 1800–1850*. Chicago: University of Chicago Press, 1968. Recent and very important. First chapter devoted to Dunlap's introduction of melodrama to the American theater.

HODGKINSON, JOHN. *A Narrative of His Connection with the Old American Company*. New York: J. Oram, 1797. Hodgkinson's side of the Hallam-Hodgkinson feud. Included in the 1963 *Theatre* reprint.

HUNT, WILLIAM S. "A Great Jerseyman—Some Aspects of William Dunlap," *Proceedings of the New Jersey Historical Society*, n.s. XII (1927), 419–24. Believes "No one has ever questioned the genius of Dunlap." Sees no faults in him. Local history.

LEARY, LEWIS. "Unrecorded Early Verse by William Dunlap," *American Literature*, XXXIX (1967), 87–88. Identifies as probably Dunlap's several poems published anonymously in the *New-York Magazine*.

McGINNIS, WILLIAM CARROLL. *William Dunlap*. Perth Amboy, N.J.: City of Perth Amboy, 1956. More local history by the City Historian: "Perth Amboy's most illustrious citizen of all time. . . . He raised many mushrooms." Gives local color.

MATLOW, MYRON. "Some Kotzebue Plays in England and America: *The Stranger* and *Pizarro*." Unpublished Ph.D. dissertation, University of Chicago, 1953. Places Dunlap among other Kotzebue translators.

MORAMARCO, FRED. "The Early Dramatic Criticism of William Dunlap," *American Literature*, XL (1968), 9–14. Discusses the "Theatrical Register" essays identified as Dunlap's in the Bowman article. Stresses Dunlap's moralism.

ODELL, G. C. D. *Annals of the New York Stage*. 15 vols. New York: Columbia University, 1929–49. Learned, genial, and intelligent. First three volumes provide much information about the New York theater of Dunlap's period.

Phillips Academy. *William Dunlap. Painter and Critic*. Andover, Mass.:

Addison Gallery of American Art, 1939. Pamphlet for centennial exhibition; comments on Dunlap as a painter and critic.

PICKERING, JAMES H. "*Satanstoe:* Cooper's Debt to William Dunlap," *American Literature,* XXXVIII (1967), 468–77. Uncovers verbal and other parallels to Dunlap's theater history and the history of New York in Cooper's novel.

QUINN, ARTHUR HOBSON. *A History of American Drama. From the Beginning to the Civil War.* 2nd ed. New York: F. S. Crofts & Co., 1943. Chapter on Dunlap (74–112) is the best short treatment of Dunlap as a dramatist, although perhaps too kind.

Review of the "Biographical Sketch" of John Vanderlyn published by William Dunlap in his "History of the Arts of Design"; with some additional notices respecting Mr. Vanderlyn, As an Artist. New York: no publisher, 1838. Pamphlet of protest by an anonymous contributor, who feels himself and Vanderlyn wronged.

RUTLEDGE, ANNA WELLS. "Dunlap Notes," *Art in America,* XXXIX (1951), 36–48. More corrections for the art history.

WEGELIN, OSCAR. *A Bibliographical Checklist of the Plays and Miscellaneous Writings of William Dunlap.* New York: Charles F. Heartman, 1916. Not always reliable and superseded by later works, but still worth consulting.

————. *William Dunlap and His Writings.* (New York: privately printed, 1904.) Very slight, but interesting as the observations of a Dunlap bibliographer.

WOOLSEY, T. S. "American Vasari," *Yale Review,* III (1914), 778–89. Favorable evaluation by a descendant, the man who kept several Dunlap diary volumes unavailable until his death. Also reprinted as a pamphlet.

Index

[159]

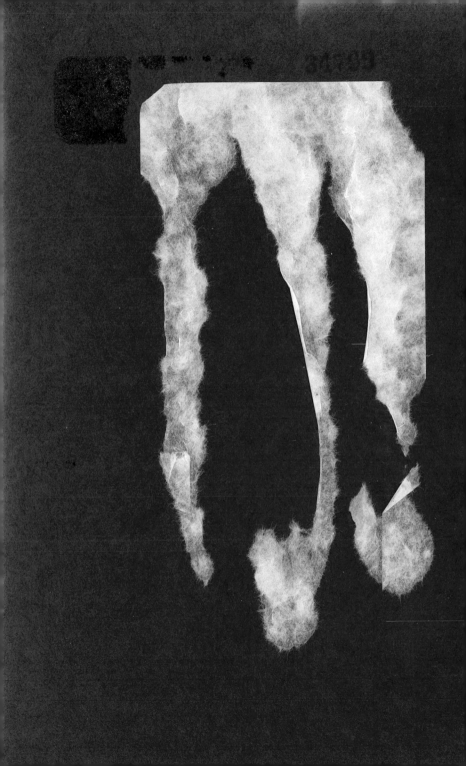